The Business of Big Data

Uri Bram & Martin Schmalz

www.thebusinessofbigdata.com

DEDICATION

This book is dedicated to C. & E.

CONTENTS

Introduction

Not too long ago, one of your authors found himself in the proverbial hipster coffee shop in Boulder, Colorado, next to a guy sipping a matcha latte and trading hundreds of millions of dollars of Bitcoin. Your author struck up a conversation, initially just curious if this person was aware of the concept of diversification, but soon more interested in how he had found himself in possession of hundreds of millions of dollars to trade from his laptop.

The answer was illuminating: marijuana had recently been legalised in Colorado, and a "green rush" of weed-entrepreneurs had flooded in to start growing and selling this green gold. Our new pal had seen this trend and realised something important: the influx of growers were going to compete away each other's profit margins until weed became one more agricultural commodity. So he started interviewing people involved in more traditional high-value crops, like blueberries in California, and asked them who in that business was sitting at the best point in the value chain. The answer was not the farmers but the warehouse-owners who stored the blueberries; our friend decided to do the same for marijuana, and shortly after found himself (wisely or otherwise) trading hundreds of millions of bitcoins from a coffee shop.

This story might illustrate a few different things about the modern economy, but an important one is simply that value is always captured by the people who think clearly and strategically about the best place in the value chain to position themselves in response to changes and developments in the economy.

The popular narrative around AI is as panicked as it is fatalistic. We certainly believe that the business of AI and big data is going to transform the economy in the coming years: we're writing a book about it, after all. But we keep meeting people who think it's too late for them — that their job is going to be replaced by a machine no matter what they do, and that the coming years will be some kind of dystopia of mass-unemployment, where everyone with a job will either be a machine learning programmer or a personal trainer for a machine learning programmer. In reality, the AI revolution will certainly bring about big economic changes (including job losses, which absolutely shouldn't be minimised); at the same time, it will bring about huge opportunities (including the opportunity to think strategically and *create* new roles and new meaning for the unemployed and underemployed).

That's why we find it strange that there's so little guidance in the public sphere right now about the economic opportunities to think creatively and strategically about the impact of AI on every different industry. While teaching a course on Big Data in Asset Management, one of your authors had two realisations: that he was suddenly in big demand to give lectures at investor conferences, and that there was no simple book helping people understand the business of big data and think strategically about how to find a place in a data-driven world. (There are plenty of books and reports about the ethical implications of big data; the antitrust implications of data-based businesses; the future of work, and the extent to which workers will be replaced by machines. We'll recommend some of our favourites at the end of the book.)

To stereotype just a little, the current environment is full of C-level executives who hear all about the importance of AI and big data and fear getting left behind. They tell their IT teams to make a data lake or a data pipeline or a data warehouse, "do some AI" on it, generally get with the programme. A few years and a few hundreds of millions of dollars later, they will survey the outcome and say "Wait… what did we do this for?" There is tragically little overlap between the economists and business people who are trained to think about strategy but don't know what the machines are doing much beyond what you can read in the newspapers, and technical people who understand what the current generation of AI is good at but aren't empowered to think about the business strategy surrounding them. This book exists to bridge that gap between basic AI and basic economics.

Depending on your line of work, the specific questions you might be asking will differ widely. If you're an investor or executive, perhaps you are thinking: should I really invest in AI firms right now? Is it a revolution, or just a fad? (You don't want to be one of those clueless C-Suiters, after all.) In which firms? There are thousands of AI companies out there. Or, how will AI transform my industry? How do I understand the business model of a tech company that doesn't have revenue, let alone profit?

If you're an engineer or entrepreneur, perhaps you're

asking: how can I get on this ride? How do I make money with AI?

If you're a student, perhaps you're wondering: what should I study right now to make sure there's good work for me by the time I graduate? If you're a regulator, maybe you're thinking: what's the right framework to think about monopoly in the world of data companies? If you're a consumer, you're asking: how does data change my relationship with my cellphone company, my supermarket, my insurer?

No matter who you are, the ultimate question is: how will this affect *me*?

This book offers a framework for all those questions based on simple economics. The logic of business models will change completely in the coming years: many markets and job-roles will be destroyed, while many others will be created; many opportunities will be presented for those who understand a little economics and a little technology, and a great deal of confusion will be sowed among those who don't. How to predict which is which? Only creative strategic thinking, strong contextual knowledge, and deep understanding of other humans can answer those questions. No computer will do it: this job is for humans. It's an excellent time for artificial intelligence, but an even better time for intelligent humans.

Chapter 1:
Why the AI Revolution Is Happening Right Now

Human Intelligence Beats Artificial Intelligence At All Non-Routine Tasks

As a researcher at the MIT Artificial Intelligence Laboratory in the late 1980s, David Chapman had a surprising realisation. While a lot of tasks that "we consider particular signs of intelligence because they are difficult for people," such as playing chess, were "easy for fast-enough computers," some tasks that are "easy for people: making breakfast, for instance," turned out to be impossibly difficult. Ultimately, "most of life is like breakfast, and very unlike chess."

There are many different kinds of AI (which can mean almost anything that we vaguely consider "intelligence" being performed by a computer), but the currently practical applications in business mostly turn around a technique called machine learning. In ML, computers learn to find patterns in a data set representing the past before being let loose on a vast pool of data the present keeps creating. Machine learning has actually been known since the 1950s, but has only become transformative in the business world thanks to the rise of big data (which, as the name suggests, is just the field of working with very large and complex datasets) and improvements in computation.

Machine learning is incomparably good at one thing: routine prediction. Routine prediction means finding patterns and making predictions in data-rich environments where the past consistently predicts the future. This is both an incredibly impressive and incredibly narrow talent. It only works in situations where we have very, very large amounts of relevant data, and where the past reliably predicts the future. While this can include tasks beyond what we would normally think of as "prediction" (one famous example is getting AI to differentiate a chihuahua from a muffin), it's still only a small fraction of what human intelligence can do.

The distinction between AI and human intelligence is something that even great minds often get wrong. When asked about AI, the (extremely intelligent) investor Charlie Munger quipped "I like the idea of using artificial intelligence because we're so short of the real thing." But artificial intelligence only refers to a very narrow skillset, whereas human intelligence refers to a very much broader one; the quip is using two different senses of the same word, like saying "I like the idea of using steam power because we're so short of political power."

Should routine prediction really be considered "intelligence" at all? That's a thorny thicket of an argument going back many decades, with some people saying that solving a problem through raw computation power shouldn't really count as intelligence, and other people saying that intelligence is always spontaneously redefined whenever machines become able to do something that everyone previously said they couldn't. This is all outside our scope here: the point is just that routine prediction is *one* small part of human intelligence, and that as machines get better at it the humans are going to do less of it. Meanwhile, human intelligence will be put to use on other tasks, especially those that help get more value out of the powers of AI.

An analogy can be made here to physical labour. As machines got better at "routine physical labour" (say, picking things up and putting things down, like a forklift or a crane or a piece of agricultural machinery), humans have come to do less and less of that kind of task across all kinds of domains and industries. But it's notable that humans have in turn started doing *more* physical labour that complements the machines, including jobs that simply didn't exist before, whether that's driving a forklift or fixing a crane or even cleaning the windows of a 50-story building that only exists because of elevators. Multiple different outcomes all happen together:

- humans stop being competitive at routine physical labour, and get replaced at those tasks by machines
- more routine physical labour gets done in total due to the machines' extra strength, opening up new opportunities and unlocking new value
- new human work gets created in tasks which complement the routine physical labour carried out by machines.

In the current technological wave, humans will increasingly be replaced by Artificial Intelligence at all routine prediction tasks, and a lot of humans currently spend a lot of their time performing routine prediction tasks. But that's only a tiny part of what *human* intelligence *can* do. Machines are still bad at a vast number of tasks that human intelligence excels at: intuition, creativity, non-generic prediction based on little data but self-developed theory, compassion, counterfactual thinking, humor, and … coming up with lists of things that human intelligence excels at…! (Seriously.) One could also say: *thinking.* This insight implies a lot about the continuing role of humans in the AI economy. We'll be talking much, much more about that later in the book.

Routine Prediction Means Extraordinary Profits

Why is routine prediction worth doing in the first place? There are three main reasons that routine prediction is (incredibly) valuable to companies who can wield it well.

The first is the obvious one: accurate prediction is always a useful skill in business, whether it's predicting how much you'll be willing to spend on a flight, how raising the price of bread will affect demand, or whether you're likely to cancel a subscription to a magazine. Since AI is much better at routine prediction than humans are, it makes more profitable decisions possible and opens up new opportunities.

For example, a good AI model transforms credit-risk assessment from an expensive and time-consuming human labour to something that a computer can do effectively in seconds. Not only does this reduce the lender's costs, it enables the lender to make loans it couldn't have made previously: whether because the sums involved were too small to justify the cost of a human evaluation, or because the lender didn't have good enough information to distinguish a risky borrower from a safer one. By reducing the cost (and risk) of lending, AI increases the viable market size.

Similarly, AI makes targeted advertising much more effective: the system can start predicting which products a customer will buy based on a thousand features of her profile, rather than the old-fashioned alternative where the advertiser can only target people at the level of "subscribers to *Fishing Weekly*." Once again, this can actually increase the market size: niche products that previously couldn't be sold at all, because they had no way to cost-effectively reach the small but enthusiastic pool of relevant consumers, can suddenly be viable businesses. AI can enable new transactions that simply wouldn't have existed otherwise.

The second reason is that routine prediction allows companies to price-discriminate between different customers. "Price discrimination" is a perhaps unfortunate term of art in economics: it means that a producer charges different prices to different consumers based on their willingness to pay. The archetypal price-discriminator is a seller at an old-fashioned market, who doesn't list prices for their products but sizes up each customer and haggles to get more money for the same goods out of any customer who is willing to pay extra.

Price discrimination allows the seller to make greater profits: one of your authors once had an entertaining conversation with a roadside statue-seller in Zimbabwe, who could rattle off the exact starting price he would quote to different customers based on their country of origin. The customers naively thought that the seller's "Where are you from?" was just small talk, but in fact he was running a sophisticated small-data price discrimination algorithm. Routine prediction allows big data businesses to price-discriminate at a much larger scale. (For example, Uber notes that you're willing to pay more for a ride if your phone battery is just about to die, though they're keen to assure consumers that they don't use this data to determine prices.)

The third reason that routine prediction is valuable is a little more subtle and complicated: for better or worse, it allows companies to unearth secret information about customers that previously would have stopped them selling to that customer at all. We'll discuss this in much greater depth in Chapter 7, but the rough version is this: an AI-armed lender might be willing to make loans to customers that a traditional bank considers too risky because the AI can use all kinds of alternative data which the traditional bank wouldn't touch. As such, better prediction creates markets that wouldn't otherwise exist.

Machine Learning, Meet Big Data

Every year, the world welcomes about 130 million new babies and 1.5 billion new cellphones. How much data do those brand new cellphones (and their slightly older cousins) generate? To have an easy time calculating, let's say each user opens 10 apps each day, and each of those apps then tracks 100 pieces of data. That's already trillions of pieces of information, and it's probably an underestimate: if you're anything like us, you've checked more than 10 apps just since starting this book.

Imagine trying to open that trillion-cell spreadsheet in Excel: Excel wouldn't just crash, it would storm out of your house muttering about unreasonable working conditions. That's one useful definition of big data: data that's too big to fit in an Excel spreadsheet.

More seriously, like so many buzzwords, big data doesn't have a single definition, but the core property of big data is simply that a dataset be large and high-dimensional, meaning that we don't just have a lot of rows in the spreadsheet but also a lot of columns — we don't just have a lot of customers, but that we also have many pieces of information stored about each customer. In the language of data, each of those columns is called a "feature", so if you hear a data scientist say "feature-rich" that's what she means.

Why would someone bother collecting all that data? In short, because large quantities of data turn machine learning from a research curiosity into a practical marvel. "The foundations of modern machine learning were developed as far back as the 1950s," says Joel Shor, a research engineer and the creator of TF-GAN, a well-known machine learning library at Google. "For many decades people stopped researching neural networks because 'they don't work.' Now, as the saying goes, they're 'unreasonably effective.' What's changed? Many researchers would agree that the *only* difference is the hardware that we use," the hardware that makes it possible to store and process truly vast amounts of data efficiently.

Now we have all the pieces to understand the AI revolution. The machine learning techniques developed in the 1950s were incredibly good at routine prediction (especially in feature-rich environments, as compared to traditional statistics), but couldn't be applied at scale without a lot more data and a lot more computation power. The development of better computation and big data technologies made it commercially viable to store enough data for machine learning to work its magic. Throughout the rest of this book, when we say "AI" we basically just mean "machine learning techniques applied on big data for the purpose of routine prediction."

This is about as different from the Hollywood image of AI as your authors are from the Hollywood image of people. This kind of AI isn't going to travel back in time to take out the future leader of a human rebellion, or overrule the commander of a human space fleet, or grind all the matter in the universe into paperclips. Whether or not that kind of AI is plausible (or possible) is another topic for other people; the point is that the kind of AI that exists *right now* is just a fancier version of statistics. This AI may be too boring for newspapers to write about, but it's full of opportunity (and is actually pretty fascinating, anyway).

Big Data Got Big Because Big Data Got Cheap

Like the latest pop sensation, you might catch yourself wondering why big data suddenly became so big. Unlike with musical trends, though, there's a simple and satisfying answer. It's all contained in this chart:

Cost of data storage 2010-2017 (USD per terabyte)

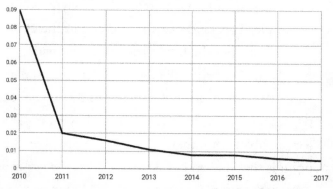

Between 2010 and 2012, the cost of storing data crashed by a factor of five. And it had been falling long before that, and kept falling afterwards. It doesn't take a genius (or even an economist) to predict that when a price falls that much, people buy and use a lot more of the thing. Indeed, the world responded to much cheaper data storage by increasing

24

its total use of data storage from 2 zettabytes in 2010 to 25 zettabytes in 2017. In 2013, IBM wrote a report saying that 90% of the useful data in the world had been generated in the last 18 months alone; in 2017, IBM wrote another report saying 90% of the useful data in the world had been generated in the last 18 months again. Of course, the figure was right both times. Data generation is increasing exponentially, so what counted as an unprecedented annual flood of data in 2013 is what we would now call "January."

We've gotten so used to the idea that data storage is "too cheap to metre" that this development might seem trivial. But it's actually crucial, and worth internalising fully. Stare at that graph until it seeps into your soul: in a single year, the cost of storing data fell by a factor of four. By comparison, in many developing countries the cost of buying a car has fallen by similarly large factors over a number of decades, and the unsurprising outcome can be seen on every road. The difference with the big data revolution is that it is happening so many times faster that we have much less time to adjust. It's no surprise that we're collectively struggling to keep up.

Positive Feedback Loops Create A Revolution

Many people justifiably wonder if the current AI wave is just a fad: so many technologies with that much hype don't live up to the breathless billing. The difference is that there's an underlying economic change — the decimated cost of data storage — that caused this particular hype, and the impact is permanent so long as storing data stays cheap. (There's no technological reason for the cost of data storage to rise, but there is a possibility that law and regulation will increase the *effective* price of storing data in some jurisdictions and change the viability of big data business models; we'll discuss that further in Chapter 6.)

But the AI wave is actually more than just the low cost of data storage combining with established machine learning techniques to make routine prediction cheap and plentiful. The reduced cost of storage has created a circle of positive feedback loops with innovation in computation and the flow of human talent into the field.

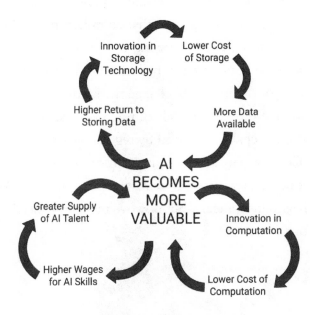

Essentially, cheaper data storage increases the returns to innovation in computation technology, and also increases the returns for talented individuals entering the field, which in turn make big data even more valuable still. This set of positive feedback loops turn the adoption of AI into a stronger and ever more powerful wave.

Of course, cheaper and better AI means cheaper and better routine prediction. As we explained at the start of this chapter, cheap and plentiful routine prediction means that humans will want (and need) to apply their intelligence in ways that complement the AI's power instead of competing with it. The rest of this book is about exactly what that shift means for you and your work: it will change the kinds of work we do and the business models of the businesses we work for, the challenges faced by regulators and the dilemmas faced by consumers (not to mention the food you eat, who you date, and your ability to get health insurance... but now we're getting ahead of our ourselves).

THE BUSINESS OF BIG DATA

Chapter 2:
Your Rideshare App Is In The Data Business, Even If You Don't Know It

Rideshares Apps Are Better Banks Than The Banks

So how does a business thrive in the age of AI? Here is a story that in recent years has recurred around the globe. A rideshare company (Uber, Lyft, Didi, GoJek, Grab, 99, Ola, you name it) starts gaining traction in its local economy. Running a rideshare app inevitably means collecting data, and the apps at first use this data merely as a side-effect of their core efforts: perhaps they use data on rider demand and driver supply to try to corral drivers into the places they're most needed. So far, so banal. Soon, this side-project creates a strong competitive advantage for the company against non-AI rivals: a traditional taxi company without a big data background, for example, isn't as good at predicting rider demand in order to deploy the right numbers of cars to the right places at the right times.

Then something happens which traditional business analysts can't make sense of: the rideshare company starts offering small loans to drivers and riders. The analysts confabulate an explanation: the loans are there to increase driver loyalty perhaps, or help prevent liquidity traps where drivers can't afford the tank of petrol they need in order to get started for the day.

What the analysts don't realise is that, like a kids' TV show character evolving into its new and more-powerful form, these businesses have transformed from rideshare companies into *data* companies. The data is the whole point of what looks like the "core business" on the surface. Since rideshare data creates an especially rich profile of its subjects (for reasons we'll see in a moment), the only question is how the company can best profit from it. Providing loans is just one of the many lucrative answers.

Let's look at one specific case. In early 2019, Chinese rideshare giant Didi Chuxing jumped into the finance business. The intent was, explicitly, "to put to work its vast trove of user data to deduce users' income from their commonly used home, office and leisure locations." Analysts said that Didi's users are "affluent and represent a quality segment of consumers for new insurance and wealth management products." Didi can infer where you live (because you travel there at night), your family and romantic connections (who you travel with and even who you visit, and where you spend your nights, based on their known home address from *their* Didi usage), what kind of job you have (based on your office address and business travel), and so on and so forth... even if you haven't told it a single one of those things explicitly. And each one of those features is an excellent predictor of whether you'll pay back a loan.

But Didi potentially knows even subtler things about you: what kind of restaurants you eat at (fast food or healthy food), whether you go out partying, whether you drink alcohol, even whether you have the self-control to wait out surge pricing and get a better fare. Feeding all of this information into an AI algorithm gives an insight on credit-worthiness that any traditional bank would salivate over... and from the customer's perspective, you get an instant decision on a loan application without (deliberately) having entered a single piece of data about yourself.

Why Your Core Business Doesn't Need To Be Profitable

In fact, an AI-savvy rideshare provider can plausibly lose money on all of its actual rides, and make the money back from its real business: the business of big data. There's an old joke about a wholesaler who sells every item at a loss. When a friend asks what the hell he's doing, he shrugs and says "We lose money on every sale, but make it up in volume." One of the niche consequences of the AI revolution is to make that joke into a plausible business model: if you make a small loss on *enough* sales, the valuable data you've gathered might suddenly be profitable enough to offset the loss.

Of course, the rules of business haven't changed, it's just a matter of incorporating a new asset (data) into the calculation. The value of a company is no longer determined by the discounted future cash flow of its traditional assets alone, it's now the discounted future cash flow of its traditional assets *plus* the cash flows its data generate. Ultimately, though, data is such an incredibly valuable asset that there will be (and actually already are) companies who make all their money from data, with their "core business" functioning solely as an elaborate data-generating machine.

The story of the rideshare companies is a perfect example of the three stages of the AI revolution.

1. In the first phase, disruptors use AI to reduce the cost of existing products. As a side effect they produce new data, which quickly turns into a side product.

2. In the second phase, data becomes the competitive advantage. The companies deploying AI here may or may not see themselves as "AI companies," but they're outracing the competition in their field because of their application of AI. A survey by Harvard Business Review Analytic Services showed that "more than half of respondents (60 percent) believe the future success of their organizations depends on using machine learning to distance themselves from competitors." Companies may switch business plans after realising the value of their data.

3. In the third phase, data becomes the point of the business model. The complementarity of data to many other products increases the value of "platforms" and "super-apps" — companies that can access (and deliver) especially rich data. At this phase, a company actually doesn't even need to be profitable in its "core" business if the data it generates is sufficiently lucrative.

The future, of course, is already here, it's just not very evenly distributed: some companies and sectors have got to Phase 3 before others have tied their shoelaces. Incidentally, it's impossible to miss that the revolution is coming to China infinitely faster than it's coming to the West — WeChat and other Chinese tech giants embody the third phase of the big data business models better than anybody else. Let's look at some case studies of companies that have successfully evolved into Phase 3 big data business models: The Lending Club, Ford, Mobike, and our friend's sushi restaurant.

How The Lending Club Reduced Fraud And Disputes Using Data

It sounds a little like a question from a child: if the interest rate that I get on my savings is hardly above 0%, but my neighbour is paying the bank for her loan at a rate of 10%, why can't I cut out the middleman and just lend my neighbour money at 5% to both our benefit?

Founded in 2007 (as one of the first Facebook Applications, in fact), the Lending Club seemingly turned that naive child's question into a business model. This company later raised almost $900 million as the largest US tech IPO of 2014, and ended its first day's trading valued at $8.5 billion.

It goes without saying that the child is missing a few things in her model of the banking business, most notably the risk of loans defaulting. But it's also true that traditional lenders add a lot of costs to the business that don't necessarily have to be there. In the United States, lenders spend on average 2.2% of each loan to pay for the branch system, an expense that can be viewed as a legacy cost rather than a modern necessity. The Lending Club spent highly on marketing, certainly, but their overall operating expenses were half those of traditional banks. Even the young child can see the benefits there.

But another interesting element of the Lending Club's advantage was that their loans had less fraud and fewer disputes than traditional banks. This might seem counterintuitive: banks are likely to have higher-quality borrowers because, frankly, most people wouldn't go to an alternative loan provider like the Lending Club unless they weren't able to get credit at their local bank first. Banks also have time-tested, stringent processes for evaluating potential borrowers. What advantage did the Lending Club have?

You guessed it: data. Instead of a loan officer looking into your eyes (and your 3-page form) and trying to get a measure of your soul (and your credit-worthiness), the Lending Club had a powerful AI model and an ever-increasing pool of data on borrowers that let it hone its predictions somewhat-closer to perfection. A loan officer in small-town America may know who your parents are and how creditworthy they were, and who your friends are — but, you guessed it, there are now many many others who know that about you, too.

How exactly can Lending Club investors, or by now pretty much any other lender, make better decisions using alternative data? The options are endless, and ever-increasing. You can create databases of known frauds and refuse to lend to them, certainly. You can examine people's debit-card spending data and use it to predict their ability to repay; in fact, you can use all kinds of spending data across all of a person's accounts to assess a borrower's creditworthiness much more accurately than an old-fashioned bank ever could. You can look at their browser history and mobile phone data (as we'll discuss in Chapter 3, you can buy off their ISP or telecom without the customer necessarily even realising).

If you're willing to be even more controversial, you can use social data about the person's network: specifically, an excellent predictor of whether you'll default on a loan than whether your friends default. The ethics of this one are very much still being debated; we'll discuss that more in Chapter 6.

You can also look at their personal habits. Here's a riddle for you: suppose a person's cellphone location data shows two different 'spikes' at night, two different locations at which they spend a significant amount of time. Are they more or less likely to pay back a loan on time, and why?

The answer is that someone with two nighttime locations is a bad credit risk, and they're a bad credit risk because they're probably having an affair (with all the financial instability that can lead to). Insiders to the industry tell us this is the second-best predictor of loan defaults after social network data. Note: the bank doesn't have this kind of data, and twenty years ago it *couldn't* have got that data without getting you trailed by a private detective out of a Raymond Chandler novel. But today an alternative lender can get this data about every single customer with trivial ease and at very low cost. Perhaps it's not so surprising that their default rates are lower than the traditional banks, and that they can therefore profit where banks fear to tread.

Ford Is Secretly A Data And Finance Firm

We know that at this point there are so many startups making noise in the data space that it's hard for even an interested person to keep up with all of them, so (strange as it sounds) you may have missed the story of a highly successful data company using innovative business models to generate (and profit from) highly valuable customer data. That company is the Ford Motor Co.

Why do we call Ford a data company? It hopefully goes without saying that Ford's original business model involved was making money by selling cars, but already one-third of their profits come from financing and loans to car dealers and drivers. Of course, the company originally entered the loan business just as a way to sell more of them. (General Motors and Alfred P. Sloan are actually said to have invented the business of consumer credit in 1919, allowing customers to receive a car with a 35% down-payment then cover the rest of the debt "on time," which the more conservative Henry Ford initially scowled at.)

But a side effect of giving these loans over decades is that Ford ended up with an extremely rich data set about every single one of its borrowers — loan applicants have to provide Ford with extensive, personal information in order to apply for their loans, and since Ford is making millions of loans in comparable conditions (for the purchase of a car) it has an excellent opportunity to use its rich trove of data and the power of AI to price the risk of different customers failing to pay off their car. Once Ford has that incredibly valuable data, there's no need to restrict itself to only using it to make car loans; at some point, producing sellable cars is merely a prelude to gathering valuable consumer data and making money from that.

Once you understand this perspective, you understand various more recent decisions by big companies that would have been decried as "empire-building" or wasteful distractions from their core business just a few years ago. For example, in 2018 Ford acquired electric scooter company Spin for $100 million. This might have seemed like an odd move: electric scooter companies seem to lose money with phenomenal prowess and reliability, and the $100 million valuation came shortly after a Series A that valued the business at only $40 million (and only a year after their first scooter hit the streets). So what exactly was Ford buying for the money?

A new trove of data, of course, along with a "data-generating" process, aka renting scooters. And why did *Ford* by it, as opposed to any other company or investor on the planet? Spin's data might be particularly well-suited (and therefore particularly valuable) to Ford, specifically: Ford has a vast trove of location data for its car-drivers, but Spin adds complementary information on additional trips those customers take by scooter. 100 million people drive Fords, so Ford might well have a better opportunity to monetise Spin data than the startup had on its own. In turn, if it continues to build up this kind of integrated data empire then Ford might now be much more valuable than the sum of its parts, and much more valuable than its currently-calculated discounted future cash flows.

The Bikeshare Business Might Only Make Sense As A Data Business

In the prestige pages of the Western press, there are beautiful-illustrated, beautifully-skeptical articles about the failure of bike-sharing in China. The colourful piles of discarded metals really do look like an accidental Jeff Koons exhibit, but is this proof of the failure of the bikeshare business or just proof that journalists don't understand it?

You can probably guess that we feel like the answer might be the latter. Bikeshare companies aren't in the bikeshare business; most of their revenue comes from selling rider data to other companies, as basically illuminated by the following two questions:

1) Have you got a ridesharing app on your phone?
2) Have you read the details of what data they collect, and what they do with it?

The business model is that for sufficiently many people the answer to 1) is "yes" and the answer to 2) is "no" (or "I don't care") and the consequences of this are that (for example) Chinese bikeshare company Mobike was simultaneously investigated by Berlin's privacy watchdog *and* purchased by Chinese web giant Meituan-Dianping for $2.7 billion. (Meituan was originally an app-based food delivery service ... which also gains valuable information about your whereabouts, by construction).

There are a couple of questions we repeatedly get asked when discussing the bikeshare business.

First, how can location data possibly be so valuable when Google and Apple, through their smartphones, *already* have everybody's location data?

It's true that the value of data depends on the willingness to pay of the highest bidder, which itself depends on the unique predictive power of your particular dataset: it's no use having a highly valuable dataset if several other companies have the exact same data to sell, and can compete your profits down to nothing. But a company can only use data they have access to, and Google and Apple aren't (currently) selling. A bikeshare company's data location data might not be as valuable as Google's or

Apple's (since those companies have many more users, and are following those users every minute of every day), but it's still location data for millions of people, and if you can't buy Apple or Google's data it's still worth a lot.

A second question we get is always accompanied by a sceptical raised-eyebrow: is it *really* plausible that someone is running an entire bikeshare business, complete with millions of physical bikes, *just* to get a user's location data?

This answer to this is rooted in the staggering disparity between costs (and profits) in the world of atoms and the world of bits. How much does it cost to mass-produce a physical bike in China? We haven't done the research, but call it $50. How much does it cost to recruit a new online banking customer? Industry reports put the number right around $500. While this is obviously an over-simplification, if it had a 10% chance of getting you to switch to their online bank, then a company would be happy to *give* you a bike for free, let alone let you share one. (Pop quiz: how much is the lifetime value of that new online banking customer?) In Chapter 7, we'll talk about insurance companies that give away Apple Watches in a similar bargain.

This is the epitome of the third stage of the AI revolution, where it's worth running a whole business just to gather useful data. The coming years will see more and more businesses that leave clueless observers scratching their heads, because they only see the external form of the business and not the data-generation operation behind it.

Even a Sushi Restaurant Can Be A Data Business

So far, this chapter might seem intimidating if you're not the sort of person who has plans to start a multi-billion dollar business. In the business of big data, will it simply be the case that only the biggest survive?

Not at all. Just because the big data business model gravitates towards scale, that doesn't mean every player in the ecosystem has to be a giant, or use the data to target ads or price discriminate, or any other of the fundamental reasons why routine prediction is useful that we discussed above. Instead, the key is simply to find a valuable point in the food chain. A very simple flashlight app, for example, can collect valuable data that another, bigger player wants access to, whether that's simply location data for every user or something more exotic. (Even more controversially, the same goes for menstruation tracking apps: they are very simple to build, and many are sharing their user's data without the user's knowledge. Users perhaps wouldn't give the data to a corporate behemoth, but don't realise that even a small friendly app is sharing their data with the behemoth anyway.)

More generally, if your goal is to benefit financially, finding the right spot in the value chain can be more important than solving a technical problem.

Here's an example. A friend of one of the authors co-founded a sushi chain, which might not initially strike you as a data driven business. The friend was good at running sushi restaurants, and soon took on Private Equity funding and started more restaurants. He realised that one of the make-or-break issues in operating his restaurants was to predict consumer demand, and therefore more efficiently allocate employee time. Employees are a *huge* cost for restaurants (generally 25-35% of revenue), and a particularly tricky one to calibrate: you don't want to have too many employees when no customers are around, but you also don't want to have too few employees when your customers are hungry. Now, is this starting to sound more like a business that might also benefit from better routine prediction?

Being who he is, our friend had in fact collected data from the very start of his operation, tracking exact customer numbers at any given time. Using AI, he was able to project his customer numbers with unusual accuracy, to the great benefit of his operation. So far, so good. He then started to think about moving from Stage 2 (data as a competitive advantage for a traditional business) to Stage 3 (where data is the core business): other restaurants clearly have the same demand-estimation problems, so perhaps he should start selling them the predictive insights gleaned from his own investigations?

But one doesn't need to stop there: what else could you use the data you got from this process for?

Demand history and estimation on a diverse set of restaurants is useful for other restaurants, sure. But it's also useful for real estate companies, who try to predict the willingness to pay of restaurant operators before their lease operations. And that number of course also . Maybe our friend the Sushi entrepreneur should start a firm selling restaurant demand data to real estate companies instead? But would he get to extract the most value there, or should he start our *own* real estate company instead?

The point here is not about what the correct answer to the question is, but that these are the correct questions to ask oneself in the age of big data. This kind of expansive thinking about data-driven business models — understanding the immense value of data, but thinking creatively and open-mindedly about where the profits from that data will accrue — will determine the difference between the people who will solve technical problems to the benefit for others and those who also gather the riches from it. It's all about sitting at the right point in the value chain, just as it was with the weed warehousing example from the introduction. So it might be well be worth some thought, don't you think?

THE BUSINESS OF BIG DATA

Chapter 3:
Everything You Do Is Data, And All That Data Is Being Tracked

Everything You Do Is Data

Every human knows that the following two interactions are not the same, even if they contain the same words in the same order:

Bob: I love you
Alice: I love you too, Bob

Bob: I love you
Alice: [long pause] I love you too, Bob

It goes without saying that at this point technology is also assessing your delays and hesitations, not to mention your words and actions. Somehow, without quite noticing, we all started walking around with a data-capturing, data-transmitting tracking devices (formerly known as mobile phones) in our pockets all day. Everywhere you go in life, you are spewing data. If you're filling in a loan application, what can the bank learn from the time it takes you to enter your ID number? Or from the number of corrections it takes you to spell your e-mail address? We'll find out later in this chapter.

As well as assessing the things you don't do, your phone is tracking your interactions with the world around you. If you pass a billboard and are interested enough to stop and read what it says, that's valuable data to the company advertising to you; some companies even track which part of the ad your eyeballs are particularly focused on. If you then go off and buy what the billboard was advertising, that's very valuable information as well. So it's no surprise that advertisers are tracking that via your phone.

In short, in a world of cellphones and AI, everything you do is data — even if it's an absence of action rather than a deliberate choice, or even if it's an interaction you're having with the non-digital environment, or even if you didn't register any data deliberately. Let's see some examples.

Why Do Companies Care About Your Location?

Why might a company (that's not in the business of transportation or spying) care about your location history? Simple: once someone knows where you spend your time, they can easily guess where you spend your money, and if they know where you spend your money they know which products to advertise to you. That's why even an app that has no inherent need for your location data — a flashlight, a stopwatch, an annoyingly addictive but completely pointless game — can profit greatly if you casually tick "accept" to all their permission requests.

Selling location data is a big business, and companies often don't need your active permission to do it. In the United States, telecom companies are legally allowed to sell your location data and so, inevitably, do. This doesn't just mean "your location data" in some aggregated, anonymised sense: given your phone number, anyone with the right know-how can get your specific phone's exact location — generally meaning, of course, *your* exact location — at this very moment.

Or how about Twitter? In 2019 there are 500,000 tweets every minute, which is quite a statistic in its own right. From 2009 until 2015, every tweet was tagged with the precise location it was sent from, available to any enquiring mind through Twitter's API. When people found out about this they complained to Twitter, who made location sharing opt-in... but not retroactively. So a vast number of Twitter users who thought they were merely giving away their insights into world affairs have also been giving away an exact history of their movements over many years to anyone interested enough to look.

Knowing where people go is valuable to companies even if it's not at the granular level of an individual phone. For many years, companies paid for aerial surveillance photos of dull-looking parking lots. What good are those photos? Well, if you know how many cars are *outside* a shop, you can guess how many people are *inside* the shop. It's true that this practice long predates AI — Sam Walton used to fly over his Walmart stores to count cars in the parking lots (presumably, also, it was fun) — but AI sure makes it easier and more effective (also less fun). Today, cellphone data has all but replaced shopping mall satellite imagery for this purpose; the data it provides is just too good to beat. But aerial surveillance photos are still used and analysed to predict crop yields, mining activity and other large-scale business activities.

What Your Browser History Says About You

The issue of telecoms selling location data is not unique; much of the data that people think is private is in fact publicly available. For example, Internet Service Providers (that is, companies such as Comcast and Verizon who sell internet connections to consumers) can legally sell their consumers' browsing histories without their knowledge. Consumers can legally opt-out, but generally don't know they were ever opted in.

What does your browser history say about you? Of course it's full of information about what you've purchased or considered purchasing, which again is of great value to advertisers, but it says a lot more, too. If you're sick and start googling your symptoms, that's of interest to a pharmacist who wants to sell you painkillers... but it's also of interest to your health insurer, and potentially to an accident and injury lawyer. (Historically, the most valuable search term on Google, determined by the cost of placing a keyword advert against it, was for mesothelioma, a rare form of cancer which personal injury lawyers can very profitably sue about.)

The most valuable data is (inevitably) the data that best ties into a company's real-world financial interests. On the consumer side, that's things like your personal spending, your probability of defaulting on a loan, or the chances you'll develop an expensive medical condition that your insurer will have to pay for. As a result, payments companies (who have direct and immediate access to some of the juiciest data about your spending) are sitting on a particularly rich seam.

What might be surprising, however, is how much payments data is publicly available too. The payments app Venmo leaves users' payment messages public by default; using that data, it's easy to identify drug dealers (who receive floods of payments with public messages saying "CBD" or the common marijuana-euphemism "trees" emoji). So not only does Venmo know what you're spending money on, so does anyone else who cares to check.

The AI Is Judging You By Your Email (And How You Type It)

It's probably not controversial to note that human beings are incredibly good at judging each other. The moment you set eyes on someone you can tell all kinds of things about them from subtle cues you might not even notice yourself noticing. Their choice of clothes, shoes, jewellery, makeup, tattoos, or hairstyle gives you lots of information not only about their taste but also about their personality, income and social class. There's no reason AI models can't start to make the same kinds of inferences. In fact, they already do.

Think about your reaction when you first see somebody's email address. You're inevitably going to make subtle inferences based on what you see, and will judge her differently if her handle is jennysmith@gmail.com versus jenmeistergeneral@gmail.com. (To be clear, those inferences are not necessarily inappropriate: if you're hiring for a job, the fact that someone would list jenmeistergeneral on her CV really might reveal relevant information about her as a candidate). But you'll also, more subtly, think differently about jensmith@gmail.com versus jensmith@hotmail.com, or jensmith@yahoo.com.

This is even more true for more obscure addresses: jennysmith@protonmail.com is presumably tech-savvy and concerned about data surveillance; jenny@jennysmith.com either runs her own business or is some kind of media figure; jenny@gmail.com was an early adopter and could sell the address for a lot of money; jenny@jenny.com was a *really* early adopter and could sell the domain for even more.

Again, where machine learning really excels is at finding patterns, regularities and predictive factors in very large data sets. So it's probably not a surprise that a computer, guided by smart humans, can be even better than a human at judging people based on their email address. A study of consumer default rates on purchases from an e-commerce platform showed that people with Hotmail and Yahoo addresses really are different:

> "Customers [whose email host was] T-online, a service that mainly sells to affluent

customers at higher prices but with better service ... are significantly less likely to default (0.51% versus the unconditional average of 0.94%). Customers from shrinking platforms like Hotmail (an old Microsoft service) and Yahoo exhibit default rates of 1.45% and 1.96%, almost twice the unconditional average."

But, for a good machine learning algorithm, judging you by your email address itself is only the start. What about judging you on the way you type your email address?

"There are [few] customers who make typing mistakes while inputting their email addresses (roughly 1% of all orders), but these customers are much more likely to default (5.09% versus the unconditional mean of 0.94%)... Customers who use only lower case when typing their name and shipping address are more than twice as likely to default as those writing names and addresses with first capital letters."

Finally, it goes without saying that (like humans), the algorithms are judging you by the device you use:

> For example, orders from mobile phones (default rate 2.14%) are three times as likely to default as orders from desktops (default rate 0.74%) and two-and-a-half times as likely to default as orders from tablets (default rate 0.91%). Orders from the Android operating systems (default rate 1.79%) are almost twice as likely to default as orders from iOS systems (1.07%) — consistent with the idea that consumers purchasing an iPhone are usually more affluent than consumers purchasing other smartphones.

The important thing to note is that these kinds of factors can have predictive power over and above the traditional characteristics they correlate with. Sure, your email provider is partly just a proxy for your age, and companies already know your age anyway. But the power of machine learning is that it can identify weird, non-linear interactions between (for example) age and email address and everything else under the sun. Your email provider has additional predictive power because it helps the system get at all kinds of personal traits that aren't revealed by existing data. Not only are Hotmail users and Gmail users different in general, but two 50-year olds are different if one is on Hotmail and one is on Gmail.

Similarly, AI can even help us predict differences in the behaviour of a *single* person at different points in time. Purchases made at 2am are fundamentally different from purchases made at 2pm, even if it's the same person doing the purchasing — most humans could make an accurate guess as to which of those cases is more likely to lead to (say) a product being returned after delivery, but of course AIs can predict that with even more accuracy.

Parents Live In Shanghai? Your Loan Is Approved

In China, peer to peer lending is a huge (and risky) business. In June 2018, regulation of the sector suddenly tightened, and more than 400 platforms collapsed in just the next three months. What did the companies that survived have in common? They were better-run and better-capitalised, of course; they also applied AI intelligently to ascertain the creditworthiness of borrowers.

Now, machine learning is particularly good at finding complex interactions between a very large number of characteristics, which often means that its success can't be captured in simple stories. But some of the "headline" findings of the p2p lenders are very interesting indeed. For example, if you are female, your probability of repaying a debt is 50% higher than if you are male. Or, if you're from Beijing, Shanghai or Shenzhen, there's a higher probability you'll repay your debt.

What might be less predictable is that if your parents are from Beijing, Shanghai or Shenzhen, you're *also* more likely to repay your debt, regardless of where you live. Why? If you fail to pay your debt, your parents are likely to take on that obligation if they're able to. Housing prices in Beijing, Shanghai and Shenzhen have risen dizzyingly in the last 15-20 years. So if your parents are from one of those cities, they'll most likely be able to cover your loan if you fail to pay it yourself.

As we'll discuss more deeply in Chapter 5, there's a huge component of human judgement and understanding in making the most of AI. The algorithm might spot that people whose parents are from those three cities have better repayment rates, but if it doesn't understand the backstory it might not extrapolate that correctly to other cities that have more recently had house price booms; conversely, without human oversight, the algorithm might be too slow to reverse that judgement if house prices in Beijing, Shanghai or Shenzhen start to falter.

Big Data Can Drive Very Big Results

Few companies have enough data to meaningfully predict the optimum price for their products in general, let alone the optimal price for each consumer. Few, but not none, and the ones that can are doing it with aplomb. "With fair accuracy, we can predict that a price reduction of a certain percentage will result in an increase in units sold of a certain percentage," said Jeff Bezos in 2006, when Amazon was fifty times smaller than it is today.

Achieving Amazon's level of data-insight requires not only "data science" skills as typically understood, but also a really exceptional understanding of economics, including how to specify and implement an effective pricing experiment and how to evaluate counterfactuals. It requires great economic theory and top-rank empirical economic work. So it's no surprise that Amazon is one of the largest recruiters outside of academia for PhD economists from top economics departments, with more than 150 economics PhDs on staff, led by a former tenured economics professor from a U.S. elite university. They work in a multi-disciplinary team with coders and data scientists, showing quite specifically how economic theory can complement AI to create vast amounts of value. (Chapter 6 talks about how.)

Of course, nothing in the world of data stays static. For now, there are only a few companies with truly big data, but even smaller companies increasingly have *access* to big data (usually through data aggregators). As some kinds of data become increasingly commoditised, who will reap the profits from them: the aggregators themselves, the companies buying the data to extract predictions from it, or someone else entirely? This is once again a question of finding the right point in the value chain, the kind of strategic thinking challenge that humans excel at, as we'll discuss in the next chapter.

Chapter 4:

Don't Compete With AI At The Things It's Good At, Complement AI With The Things You're Good At

Don't Fight The Ox-Power

Imagine you're a farmer in the very distant past: your grandfather turned the soil with his bare hands, and your mother, the famous inventor, tied a stick onto a rock and invented the hand-drawn plough. You have always been admired for your muscular physique, and from a very young age you pulled the stick-plough across the fields all day and ploughed so fast that it made your grandfather cry. (Does it need to be said that this is not an accurate history of agriculture? It is not an accurate history of agriculture.)

Then one day your annoying little sister has an idea: after a family squabble where she says that you are "basically just a big fat ox-face," she marches out to the fields and ties the hand-drawn plough to an ox instead. Despite your best efforts, the ox is in fact a better plough-puller than you are. You can already see that you are not going to have a future in this business; in a few years' time, all human plough-pulling will be replaced.

Yes, this is not a particularly subtle metaphor: the ox is a stand-in for AI's "routine prediction" power.

One thing to note, here, is that the arrival of the ox-drawn plough puts specific people out of work *even though* it creates a huge amount of value in the long run. The nightly news broadcast from your local town crier will probably shout about the obvious, immediate consequence of the newly capable oxen: human plough-pullers are going to lose their jobs. This is not at all wrong, and it's very important, but it's also only half the story, and the decidedly more depressing and less exciting part. We understand why it makes the headlines — it generates fear. Also, it takes less effort to understand: the visible, direct consequences of a technological change will always be easier to predict than the less-visible, more-subtle ones, because it doesn't need creativity — but the other half of the story is just as important, and (crucially) more immediately valuable if you are one of the people whose hard-won skills are suddenly supplanted by technology. As a former hand-plougher you can do one of three things:

1) Move into a profession which oxen are bad at: painting, or planting flowers, for example.
2) Learn to drive an ox-team.

3) Spend your time creatively coming up with clever ways to deploy ox-power and increase the profits from the ox-conomy.

Let's look more at each of those options

Do Something That AI's Can't

A fun and memorable local experience while travelling is going to get a haircut. (If you've recently seen the co-author of this book with the decidedly schmaltzier last name, you'd likely conclude he should travel more in the hope it'll result in a haircut.) No matter where you go in the world it's always possible to vaguely mime the idea "cut my hair a bit" and have a memorable local experience. In Bali, a hairdresser insisted that one of your authors perform a karaoke number before leaving the salon, a video of which may be circulating in Indonesia with the title "Foreigner Sings Badly."

These experiences highlight a core fact about cutting hair: it's an intensely human activity. The physical act of hairdressing is a big challenge already because every head of hair is different, making it hard to create a robot that can manage the "terrain", but more importantly hair-cutting requires a sense of aesthetics and counterfactuals ("what would this customer look like with a different style?"), and the job of a hairdresser is about more than cutting hair: it also includes making the customer feel comfortable and pampered, listening to their gossip or complaints, or nudging them into singing for the crowds.

Since AIs are only good at routine prediction (finding patterns in data-rich environments where the past predicts the future), you can avoid being replaced by AI simply by working in the *opposite* environment: data-sparse, non-generic, where each case is in some ways unique. Hairdressing is a fine example, and becoming a hairdresser in the age of AI is like becoming a painter in the age of the ox: you might not get direct practical benefits from the new technology, but you also won't be replaced by it.

Now contrast the hairdresser with a London cab driver. Until quite recently, the achievements of the cabby — memorising every street in the city to pass a three-year exam that is literally called *The Knowledge* — were rightly applauded as incredible feats of human mental agility. The value of The Knowledge, however, has been decimated in the last decade because estimating the best route from A to B is a gold-standard simple prediction task that can now be done easily by anyone with GoogleMaps. There is still a lot of work for drivers, and the human part of the role (good conversation, dealing with exceptional situations) is still very much appreciated. But The Knowledge is no longer a premium skill the way it was.

There's a certain human temptation to look at life as a sort of morality play: we want virtue to be rewarded, hard work to lead to good results. For better or worse, the universe simply doesn't work that way. To say that The Knowledge has been outcompeted by AI is no more a knock on the cabbies' mental achievements than the fact that impressively-strong humans were long ago replaced by forklifts for heavy lifting. These are simply tasks that machines do better than we do, no matter how impressive our efforts.

Within A Single Job There Are Many Tasks

How about radiology? Among other responsibilities, radiologists spend a lot of time examining medical images (x-rays, ultrasounds, MRIs and so forth) to diagnose whether a tumour is cancerous or not. This is obviously important, prestigious, well-paid work. But it's also a clear case of routine prediction. There's a vast amount of image data from previous tumours, and it's known whether or not those tumours were cancerous. The images are incredibly "feature rich," and may have very subtle differences that help predict cancerousness which are invisible to the human eye. Biology being what it is, we are confident that the "past predicts the future" and that cancerous tumours today will look like cancerous tumours yesterday. In short, this is a gold-standard routine prediction task, so AIs will inevitably out-perform humans at routinely assessing cancerous tumours.

It's important to stress that the relevant question is which *tasks* will get replaced by AI, not which *jobs*. Human judgement will always be needed to complement AI: in radiology, for example, a human might still need to check the AI's work, perhaps to look for egregious errors or to make treatment recommendations based on the AI's prediction. A human will probably do much of the communicating with patients. The value of the human's work will actually go up: she might get paid even more than current radiologists do, because thanks to the help of the machine, she now can do her job much more efficiently and create more value in less time. In fact, by letting the AI take over the routine prediction part of the work, doctors may finally have more time for their patients again, to treat their unique symptoms and sufferings holistically.

A similar dynamic exists between different jobs within a single industry. High Frequency Trading is not only highly automated, but even the automation isn't done by "finance people": Renaissance Technologies, one of the most successful hedge funds ever, was founded by the former MIT mathematics professor, and hires mainly mathematicians and computer scientists. Meanwhile, global macro funds — who make their investment decisions based on the macro political and economic climates in different countries — remain dominated by humans that use intuition (along with analysis). What's the difference?

Well, High Frequency Trading is a classic routine prediction task: floods of data with a very long history where the past predicts the future, and the victor is the company that can write the best algorithms to profit from it. There are trillions of datapoints for Microsoft stock trades, and there's no way for a human to deal with all that data, so machines do it instead. At this point, very little trading involves a human on either side of the deal.

By contrast, since the environment is far more data-sparse and much less easily interpretable, a macro fund manager has to use her judgement to understand a complicated and un-modellable environment. None of the current AI tools can do what she does.

Ultimately, the question is only which *tasks* within a given field will get executed by machines and which will get executed by humans, and so which *skills* humans should continue cultivating and which we should give up on entirely.

Learning To Code Is A Great Idea, But You Don't Have To Become A Coder

The second way to work with the ox-revolution was to learn to drive an ox-team: instead of pulling the plough yourself, you learn how to make the ox pull the plough for you. In the case of AI, that means learning to code.

Learning to code is a great idea, but that doesn't necessarily mean becoming a coder. It's true that in 2019 there are incredibly high incomes being made by AI programmers, sometimes straight out of bootcamps that in nine months take a student from total novice to competent practitioner. In fact, that flood of talent into the field might be a problem, if you're getting into AI programming for the payoff. The current generation of AI programmers has benefitted from the relatively sudden arrival of the revolution, and so the high demand from businesses for the small pool of people who already have the required skills.

But any skill that is simple to learn and lucrative to deploy will quickly be learned by many people, and in the long run the pay will stabilise. (How long the long run is depends on how fast demand for programmers will increase relative to the supply.) Knowing how to drive a car may have been super lucrative in the brief time when cars came in and few people knew how to drive them, but in the long run the ability to drive became a commodity. Ultimately, the ability to *implement* AI algorithms — while certainly not trivial — is also not a superpower: applying AI might seem intimidating at first, but you can achieve a vast amount (with very little understanding) by using ready-made tools from the likes of Google and Amazon. (You can also take a class one of us developed for Oxford MBA students.) If you can't (or won't) do that yourself, you can pay someone else to use those ready-made tools for you, and the number of people who can successfully do so increases every day.

But even for those who aren't going to code in their day to day lives, knowing *how* to code (to a basic level) if an incredibly useful skill. In order to deploy AI effectively, strategic decision makers within any organisation need to know what machine learning can and can't do, and there's no better way to do that than to have some direct personal experience of its strengths, limitations and opportunities. It's probably no coincidence that the likes of Satya Nadella and Sundar Pichai were respected engineers before they were made chief executives of the world's biggest tech companies, despite the fact that they no longer make daily commits to the codebase. As more and more companies become (fundamentally) data companies, the best opportunities will increasingly go to strategic thinkers who have enough technical understanding to figure out how to make the most of AI. That's the topic of our next chapter.

Chapter 5:
Super Humans, Or The Unique Human Intelligence Strengths That Complement AI

Human Intelligence For Fun And Profit

Whether you know it or not, you've actually been labouring elegantly alongside AI for the last few years to create an output that neither you nor AI could manage alone. Both of you make use of your unique strengths, and combine them to create a vast amount of value. How could you be working alongside AI without even realising? The answer is reCAPTCHA, the weird little challenges you have to answer every time you submit details at a website and it asks you to prove you're not a robot by doing a little task that robots can't do.

You may have thought that your "work" on those challenges was simply make-work — that the websites were simply giving you a task that machines couldn't manage. But the system is actually much cleverer than that: reCAPTCHA is part of a massive effort to digitise books. AI is able to do the vast majority of the work: scanning and digitising clearly-printed text is a classic routine prediction task. But whenever the machine hits a piece of text that is smeared or smushed or otherwise indecipherable, it sends the image over to reCAPTCHA, where a human like you will use your unique human traits (context awareness, creativity and intuition) to figure out what the messy text actually says.

Together, you're able to do something that neither of you could do alone. The human effort required to digitise *all* books without machine assistance would be so vast as to be impossible; at the same time, the machines aren't able to go the last mile and figure out the text in the most difficult contexts. But working together, the human-machine team is able to create an extraordinary amount of value (making all books instantly searchable online, a dream that past generations could not have hoped for).

The story of reCAPTCHA is the story of our future, as humans and machines: finding ways that our uniquely human traits can complement the machine's great skills at routine prediction. That's what this chapter is all about.

First, even as "routine" AI coding becomes more commoditised, cutting-edge AI research will continue to be incredibly lucrative as the frontier pushes outwards. If you're a mathematical programming genius who can apply difficult human intelligence to improve the AI tools that are used by the rest of the world, you're certainly complementing AI in a highly creative and valuable way.

Second, an excellent way to harness the power of AI is to manage the people implementing it. Currently, many of the people leading teams of data scientists at big tech companies are PhD economists and statisticians — but if there's one main reason to get a PhD in statistics it's because you're the sort of person who doesn't want to manage a team. Which leaves a big opportunity for people with skills in management who also bother to get a proper understanding of coding and the economic value of AI (as, of course, you're doing in this book). Being a "translator" between the engineering and business teams is going to remain a uniquely human ability, and very lucrative.

Third, a key role for humans complementing AI is "understanding and analysing the role of humans complementing AI." This may sound like some kind of koan but it's a deeply important truth. As new AI tools get developed — and as more and more competitors implement existing AI tools — figuring out which existing tasks in any given business are substitutes for AI, and which are complements, creates new value again and again. It might be titled "economic theory", or it might be titled "corporate strategy", but the task of understanding the role of humans in the world of AI is one that only a human can perform. (The AI revolution hasn't happened before, so the task at hand is clearly not a routine prediction.)

Looking at things from the AI's point of view, one thing AI is really bad at is predicting "what will be the economic impact of AI?" We've said non-stop that AI's superpower is routine prediction, which only works in domains where we have a lot of data and where the past predicts the future. But AI hasn't happened in the past, so AI can't predict what the impacts of AI will be. This is a classic task for human intelligence: look at previous technological waves and their impact on society, examine the current strengths and weaknesses of AI, and use good human judgement to make predictions despite the uncertainties.

Good Theory Saves Planes

As a Hungarian Jew, Abraham Wald had been forced out of Austria in 1938. As part of the Statistical Research Group at Columbia University, he had the chance to use his phenomenal mathematical prowess to contribute to the war effort. But first he had a problem to solve. American airplanes were returning from missions over Europe with serious damage, and the military had gathered data about which parts of the plane were most likely to come back riddled with bullets. It turned out the fuselages had 50% more bullet damage than the engines, which the military took to mean that the fuselage should be reinforced more. (The reason they couldn't simply reinforce the whole plane was that armour makes the plane heavier, and therefore less nimble and fuel-efficient.) They came to Wald to ask him to calculate exactly how much extra armour should be put on the fuselage.

No, Wald told them, your data doesn't imply what you think it does. You ought to put extra armour on the *engines*. The sample of planes that make it back to camp is not the relevant one; the important sample is that planes that never returned. What you really wanted to know was where the planes that *never* returned had been hit. But you're not able to look at them, because they never came back. To Wald, the fact that fewer returning planes had bullet-holes around the engine implied that a bullet to the engine area was much more dangerous and more likely to cause a plane not to return at all, whereas a bullet to the fuselage was much more likely to be a survivable inconvenience.

Wald worked many decades before the AI revolution, but we think we can say with confidence that if he were working now he would have been someone who unlocked vast value from the power of AI. The kind of human intelligence Wald deployed was exactly the kind that best complements AI's powers of routine prediction: he used creativity, originality and wise understanding of context to analyse existing data in a different way and draw a better conclusion than other people did.

We believe that the human strengths that complement AI can generally be surmised in one word: theory. Data doesn't exist in a vacuum, and drawing good conclusions from data (and from machine learning algorithms let loose on big data) is always a question of applying theory correctly to a given situation.

It might surprise you to hear us — as economists and statisticians — praising theory "over" data, but the people who slavishly worship data on its own have always confused us. It's certainly true that, as AI makes data analysis cheaper, a lot more data analysis will get done. The mistake is to think that this means *all* theory will get replaced by data analysis, or that theory will lose all its value. Nobel Laureate econometrician Lars Peter Hansen put it well when he said that "data seldom, if ever, speaks for itself." A lot of human intelligence is needed to extract the wisdom that is lost in information. To quote Charlie Munger, "You can't really know anything if you just remember isolated facts and try and bang 'em back. If the facts don't hang together on a latticework of theory, you don't have them in a usable form." As machines get better and better at helping with the "facts" side of things, the value of good theory rises rather than falls.

AI Can't Tell You When Not To Apply AI

In fact, any time a decision is needed about whether past data is or isn't relevant to a new situation, human intelligence is needed before AI can be let loose with its routine prediction power. For example, suppose a war breaks out between the US and China. Will it be similar or different from the wars of the past? There's a case to be made that it's a structural break, and that the history of previous wars tells us nothing about what will happen in this one. There's, equally, a case to be made that we've had a lot of wars in our history, and that the previous wars will surely predict *something* about the next one. Whichever player is actually right about this will have a very prosperous future.

A lot of the interesting questions that we collectively consume our time with share this trait: it's just not clear that previous data applies, or in which ways previous data applies. Will the current President (or Prime Minister, or Chairperson, or whatever else) win re-election? We certainly have data about previous elections, and know some factors that historically predicted whether a candidate won an election or not.

But there always seem to be special factors that make people feel that the current President or the current election are somehow different. Are those differences actually relevant, or are they already baked into routine statistics (favourability and unfavourability numbers, or economic conditions) that have also applied in previous elections? It's a judgement call every time, and one that requires human intelligence.

If you're running (say) an algorithmic trading firm, the answer to these questions matters a lot. You've set up your computers in a particular way and left them humming to make you money. So long as the right conditions apply — so long as we have a lot of relevant data from applicable situations — this is a perfectly sensible strategy. But when some fairly large and unusual event happens (a surprise presidential election, an unprecedented terrorist attack, the Brexit referendum) you need to decide whether or not to turn off the computers to prevent them making stupid trades. Is this just another day like the days before it, where the machines can keep making money based on routine prediction from past trends, or is this a structural break that requires "starting again" on the data-gathering before making good predictions again? Once again, this is a matter for human intelligence to handle: AI can't advise you when not to use AI.

Collecting And Preparing Data Is 80% Of The Work

Of course, data doesn't just arrive like manna from heaven. One of your authors experienced this first-hand while working on the analysis of an education project. The goal was to look at aggregate student outcomes from different academic courses and see which ones caused the best improvements in student outcomes. So far, so noble. But after getting started on the project, your author discovered that for "privacy reasons" the project owner was planning to delete the data from any course that had fewer than 10 students. Did that decision make sense in the context?

Until now, we've been implicitly playing into a common false narrative: that datasets are a "given," and that the problem is just deciding how to analyse the data that is already there. But it's hard to exaggerate the extent to which doing anything meaningful with data requires getting a human with actual understanding of the domain to collect, clean and organise the relevant data before AI can be let loose on it. IBM's Arvind Krishna says that "80% of the work with an AI project is collecting and preparing data," and that a lot of companies bail "because you spend your first year just collecting and cleansing." Collecting and cleaning data is another crucial application of human intelligence.

Similarly, political and sports stats guru Nate Silver says that "if you want to be a good data scientist, you should spend ~49% of your time developing your statistical intuition (i.e. how to ask good questions of the data), and ~49% of your time on domain knowledge (improving overall understanding of your field). Only ~2% on methods per se." Statistical intuition and domain knowledge are relevant exactly because all the decisions about which data to collect and which questions to ask of it require real understanding of what the data means and how it should be cared for.

In the case of the student outcomes project, the privacy concern might be reasonable on its own terms, but deleting the data from all small courses is dangerous for the analysis: the kind of course that gets very few students is not representative of courses more generally, whether because small courses are highly selective, or because they're unpopular, or because they're niche. Every one of those hypotheses is a result of human intelligence and domain knowledge, on understanding which data is relevant to a given question and how to respond when some of that data is missing (or needs to be protected). A computer can't do these things because it has no human-style intelligence. The data it receives is just data, to be churned and returned for whatever it means. It's the human that supplies the meaning.

AI Doesn't Understand Cause And Effect

Watching AIs go wrong can be pretty funny. One of your authors published a book in 2013, with a new edition in 2017: humans naturally saw that there was a new edition on the market and so bought it instead of the old one, and the original seller stopped supplying the old one, knowing there would be no demand for it. The human participants in the market had all applied their human intelligence so naturally that they surely didn't give it a second thought.

By contrast, various second-hand booksellers on Amazon use automated bots to price their wares. Those bots noticed a sudden decrease in supply for the recently-popular 2013 edition, so at the time of writing there are three bots trying to sell it for $196, $996 and $3,065 (while the human-priced 2017 edition sells for $10).

A human could look at this situation and see the absurdity, but to an AI no price is really more absurd than any other, so human intelligence is desperately needed as a complement to AI's superpowers. In this case, the human superpower is the ability to distinguish cause from effect. If there's one statistics dictum every lay-person has heard it's that "correlation is not causation", but your friendly neighbourhood AI hasn't heard any dictums at all.

In the second-hand book case, what might have happened is that the AI saw a pattern where scarcity goes with high prices: it might therefore routinely predict that if the supply of a particular good is low then the price should be jacked up. However, this fails to distinguish cases where supply is scarce and demand is high from cases where supply is scarce because demand is non-existent (in this case, because a product has become obsolete).

This, incidentally, is one of those situations which highlights the complementarities between data scientists and economists. A data scientist can write an algorithm that spots patterns in supply and price, and therefore tries to sell a now-obsolete book for $3,065 simply because there are other "rare books" on the market which merit a high price due to their scarcity. But she can also write an algorithm that behaves differently, that incorporates more theory, and it's her colleague the economist who can help understand which theories might apply in a particular situation (or run experiments that tease out the causal structure of a particular environment). This kind of work brings together all the human traits that are most useful in complementing AI: good economic logic and conceptual thinking, but also creativity and context knowledge and working well in a team.

THE BUSINESS OF BIG DATA

Chapter 6:
How Law And Ethics
Constrain AI Business
Models

Law and Ethics Constrain Which Business Models Are Possible

Of course, the possible business models of big data (and the possible roles for humans within them) are not just constrained by technology but also by law and ethics. As with many other fields, such as genetics, we have to think about not only whether we *can* do something but also stop to question whether we *should*. And this becomes an even more fraught topic in an international context, where different jurisdictions come to different conclusions about what's allowable, and therefore different opportunities for what is possible.

For example, in 2019, serious political impetus to break up Big Tech started gathering momentum in the highest reaches of American media and politics. "Today's big tech companies have too much power — too much power over our economy, our society, and our democracy" wrote Senator Elizabeth Warren. "They've bulldozed competition, used our private information for profit, and tilted the playing field against everyone else."

You might be wondering how Facebook feels about this, and Mark Zuckerberg is happy to tell you: if you break up Facebook, "the alternative, frankly, is going to be the Chinese companies. If we adopt a stance [that as a country] we want to clip the wings of these [American] companies and make it so that it's harder for them to operate ... then there are plenty of other companies out [there] that are willing and able to take the place of the work that we're doing... [Specifically the Chinese companies]. And they do not share the values that we have."

Both sides of this argument nicely illustrate the powerful (and unavoidable) intersection between business, law and ethics. Businesses don't exist in a vacuum: legal and regulatory regimes always determine which business models are viable and which are impossible. (At an early stage, Uber was worth either billions of dollars or zero dollars depending entirely on whether it could eventually convince legislators that its business model was legal.) And the legal constraints on businesses work very, very differently in different jurisdictions: Facebook is worth over $500 billion as we write this, but it would be worth even more under a laxer legal regime for data, and worth much less under a stricter regime (say, if targeted advertising were made illegal).

Anyone seeking to create value in the age of AI needs to think carefully about their own beliefs on the ethical limits on the use of data, and the societal beliefs that will ultimately create the legal and regulatory limits on any kind of business model.

This Is How AdTech Actually Works

It's worth taking a moment to understand why Facebook's business model is so tied to data and data-privacy: Facebook makes 98% of its revenue from advertising ($16.6 billion out of its $16.9 billion total in the last quarter of 2018). Digital advertising is a winner-takes-most market: Facebook and Google receive over 60% of U.S. digital advertising spending, and the biggest change in the market in 2018 and 2019 was the rapid rise of Amazon into third place. It's not a coincidence that the behemoths are dominating the advertising business, but the reason these companies can offer the best value for advertisers is not *just* their size but the quality of their data.

Imagine you're selling a niche product with a $10 profit margin. Let's say it's an elbow-protector for people with especially sensitive elbows. You're therefore willing to spend up to $10 to reach a new buyer. The local newspaper is happy to run your advert, of course, but you know that most of the readers won't be interested — you expect that only 1 in a million people in the general population is interested in extra elbow protection. As a result, you're only willing to pay the newspaper $10 divided by a million, or 0.001 cents per reader.

Facebook, on the other hand, allows you to directly target people who are specifically likely to be interested in your product: people who have whatever demographic predictors exist for elbow troubles, or perhaps even people who have posted a status like "fell down and hurt my elbows again :(Will nobody help protect the sensitive-elbowed individual?" (Meanwhile, Google can target adverts to people who have googled the question "how to protect sensitive elbows?", and Amazon can target people who are literally shopping for elbow protectors.) Better data means infinitely better outcomes: if Facebook can show your advert to an audience where 1 in 1,000 viewers will actually buy your product, you're willing to pay Facebook 1,000 times more per viewer than you were willing to pay the local newspaper.

This rather simple insight is basically everything you need to know about AdTech. It's why Facebook is worth billions and your local newspaper is going bust; it's why ad-consumers on mobile are more valuable than ad-consumers on desktop (because mobile profiles tie together more data, and are therefore even richer targets); it's why Facebook would love to bundle together your separate profiles on WhatsApp, Instagram, Facebook and whatever other companies they acquire in future to squeeze out even more relevance in its targeting. The richer the user-data Facebook has, the more specific and therefore more lucrative their advertising will be. While some of the limitations on data-bundling are technical or financial, many others come down to what the law will and won't let companies do. That's why data regulation matters, and why differing data regulation regimes will lead to different outcomes.

Google And Mastercard Together Know Exactly Whether Ads Work

WeChat is the "everything platform" for Chinese mobile devices, where users do everything from booking a doctor's appointment to paying their taxes to, you know, actually chatting. WeChat's data is almost comically valuable: since people in China do everything on WeChat, WeChat can collate the data about every different type of lucrative consumer behaviour. The sum is greater than the already-lucrative parts.

Every Western tech company would like to be WeChat, and none of them have managed it, so they're settling for second-best: pulling together consumer data from many different areas through partnerships between companies.

For example, in Chapter 3 we discussed the value of personalised location data in figuring out whether a particular advertisement led to a sale: if you see an advert for a particular product and then enter a store which sells that product, we can guess somewhat-reasonably that the advert led you to purchase the product. But it would clearly be much better to know not just where you shopped but exactly what you bought. Who has *that* data right now?

Your credit card company, of course, but *they* don't have data on the online ads you've seen. That's why, unbeknown to most of their combined users, Google cut a deal with Mastercard to tie online advertising to real-world purchases. Google knows exactly which adverts you've seen; Mastercard knows exactly what you buy, and the combination of those two kinds of data is more valuable than either one alone.

Is Pooling Data An Abuse Of A Dominant Position?

Merging data from different apps is a whole new frontier in (anti)-competitive behaviour that regulators are still struggling to tame. Facebook purchased both WhatsApp and Instagram, promising not to merge user data across the three platforms despite the fact that many users simultaneously have accounts on two or three of them. Facebook later changed its mind. The combined entity is not a monopoly in the traditional sense: anyone can start a messaging app to compete with Facebook's Messenger and WhatsApp, or a photo app to compete with Instagram, or a general social network app to compete with Facebook. But the combined network effects of the three apps together give Facebook a moat that is very hard for new entrants to cross.

As a result, the German competition authority — the *Bundeskartellamt*, or Federal Cartel Office — has stepped in to prohibit the joint use of data between Facebook, WhatsApp and Instagram. Other regulators have been slower to act and seem to be going for the old "wait and see" technique, though as with un-mixing purple paint it's not clear how the datasets could be disentangled once they are fully combined.

Competition-related responses to Facebook's data policies are separate from privacy-regulation issues which are increasingly prominent in the public conversation about Big Tech. The Competition Authority specifically has no power to defend user's privacy for its own sake — that's a matter for some kind of privacy regulator (such as GDPR in the EU). Perhaps users don't like companies combining seemingly-separate data about them from multiple sources; perhaps they feel that it happened without their consent, even if they did sign the old lie *I have read the Terms and Conditions.* That's all well and good, but it's a matter for GDPR and not the competition authority.

What the *Bundeskartellamt* is alleging (and regulating) is something else: that the lack of competition in the sector means users actually have nowhere to go to get a more-private social network even if they want one. It's not illegal to have a monopoly; it's illegal to use the *power* that comes with a monopoly (known in Germany as Abuse of a Dominant Position). The *Bundeskartellamt* ruled that Facebook is abusing its dominant position by offering a low-privacy product, so the regulator will step in and change how Facebook operates. This is a new frontier for competition authorities, and will only get more important in the years ahead: what counts as Abuse of a Dominant Position in the age of big data?

The Data Is Public, But May Not Be Analysed

The frontiers of data regulation are still being fought over and developed, and the next few years will be a particularly sensitive time. There is increasing awareness of the possible applications of big data, and yet many of those applications are still nascent and so can still be killed before they grow.

For example, for as long as there have been highly-paid law firms and expensive litigation, there have been sad young lawyers staying up all night to comb through hundreds of previous cases to predict how susceptible a particular judge is to different kinds of arguments or allegations that the more senior lawyers want to make. It goes without saying that this is just the kind of task that an AI can do as well as if not better than a human can, and infinitely faster (and we're not even sure in this case if the humans being replaced are actually upset about it).

Except, in France, they've now been banned. French cases are generally published publicly and transparently, so the relevant information is already out there, but analysing it is now illegal: the 2019 Justice Reform Act declared that "the identity data of magistrates and members of the judiciary cannot be reused with the purpose or effect of evaluating, analysing, comparing or predicting their actual or alleged professional practices." The move was directly aimed at the "litigation analytics" firms already doing exactly that.

There's an old trope that every decision can be explained by both a high-minded philosophical reason and a petty personal one. The petty personal reason to ban legal AI seems quite straightforward: judges "didn't like how the pattern of their decisions — now relatively easy to model — were potentially open for all to see" and feared that the fully-analysed statistical patterns in their decisions "may reveal too great a variance from expected Civil Law norms."

Using AI To Predict Recidivism Rates

Perhaps the biggest AI fairness controversy so far has been around COMPAS, the prediction tool for recidivism rates among the recently incarcerated.

COMPAS is an AI used to predict whether an offender will recidivate after being released… which means that it's used to help decide *who* gets released, which of course has a huge impact on both the millions of incarcerated people (an algorithm is determining whether they'll go free or not) and on the whole population of the country.

Given the disparities in incarceration rates by race — black men are about eight times more likely to be incarcerated than white men — people rightly wondered whether COMPAS is fair.

So, is COMPAS fair?

Well... it seems to do a good, though imperfect, job of predicting recidivism. If you bucket the COMPAS predictions into ten groups, from highest predicted likelihood of recidivation to lowest, each group is indeed less likely than the last to be re-arrested after release. What's more, if you do the analysis separately for black and white people at each of those risk levels, black and white defendants had statistically similar re-arrest rates. Stated like that, COMPAS seems reasonably fair.

However, there's another way to look at things. In practice, a much higher share of black defendants are put in the high risk group (3/5th of black defendants) while a much lower share of white defendants are declared to be high risk (1/3rd of white defendants). As a result, COMPAS' false positive and false negative rates for black defendants were significantly worse than for white defendants: 45% of black defendants who were predicted to recidivate in fact did not, while only 24% of white defendants who were predicted to recidivate did not. Meanwhile, 48% of white defendants who were predicted not to recidivate actually did, while only 28% of black defendants who were predicted not to recidivate actually did.

On average, then, black defendants were almost twice as likely to be wrongly "accused" of being likely to commit crimes in future, *and* white defendants were almost twice as likely to be wrongly "cleared" of being likely to commit crimes in future. (Both "accused" and "cleared" seem like the wrong terms for crimes that haven't been committed yet, but we don't yet have better vocabulary for "probabilistic pre-crime.") Stated like that, COMPAS doesn't seem so fair.

So who's right about COMPAS, the critics or the defenders ? The answer is "both": it just depends on one's definition of fairness. There are five different kinds of errors that COMPAS could be measured by:

- Probability that someone is predicted to recidivate *given* that they ultimately don't
- Probability that someone is predicted not to recidivate *given* that they ultimately do
- Probability that someone recidivates *given* that they were predicted not to
- Probability that someone survives *given* that they were predicted not to
- Overall misclassification rate (that is, the previous four categories all together)

You can try to minimise any one of these rates, but you can't minimise all of them simultaneously. It might be possible to create an algorithm that was demonstrably *un*fair, that treated black defendants worse by *all* possible criteria. But you can't create an algorithm that's *fair* by all reasonable standards at once.

Of course, this is true for human decision-makers too: it's also impossible for *their* decisions to be fair by all reasonable criteria, since they face the same mathematical constraints that COMPAS and other algorithms do. The difference is that each of the human decision-makers tends to operate at a small scale, making it harder to rigorously assess the biases in their assessments. The AI does explicitly what the humans do implicitly, so there's a more direct conversation to be had about which standards of fairness ought to be applied. Finally, we react differently to human bias and AI bias — we have a social agreement to act as if human judges (and other human decision-makers) are always and everywhere impartial, whereas in fact human decision-making is notoriously flawed and fallible. The rise of AI will lead to new regulations, laws and ethical quandaries, but sometimes those quandaries will also force us to rethink how we assess human decision-making, too.

Chapter 7: Are Insurance Markets About To Self-Destruct?

Bringing It All Together: Insurance Case Study

In the short span of this book we've covered a lot of topics: we began by explaining how machine learning's superpower is routine prediction, and how big data created the perfect space for machine learning to run riot in and create new value (and new challenges) for businesses. We talked about the three phases of the AI revolution, and how business models shift from "traditional" business to focus on data. We explored how phones and other devices mean that everyone is being tracked all the time, even when they're not deliberately submitting data, and how law and ethics are sometimes the only constraints on which data can or can't be used in a routine prediction setup.

Now we're going to look at all those questions in the context of one specific case study: insurance. Perhaps it's not surprising that insurance has been at the forefront of the AI revolution: it's an incredibly lucrative business, with vast amounts of data, in which the name of the game is to find patterns between customers and predict the future based on the past. It's also the perfect case study to tie together the conceptual tools we've developed throughout the book.

In fact, the insurance market takes us into entirely new territory: the shifting power dynamics between consumers and producers in a world where the producer knows more about the consumer than she knows about herself.

The Twin Evils of Insurance

Like so many unfortunate people before him, one of your authors has a brother (a twin, in fact) who is basically better than him in every way: our twin eats better, exercises more, and makes better life choices. It's important to note that, until recently insurance companies couldn't tell the difference between us: we have the same date of birth, the same genes, and the same family medical history. But that's all changing in the age of AI.

The principle of insurance is as simple as the practice is difficult. In theory, insurance should be a wonderful thing: every one of us is at risk of freak events that are 1) rare, 2) beyond our control, and 3) so big that we can't or don't want to personally handle them financially. If we pool together with millions of others, the collective fund is enough to cover those rare losses, and we're all willing to pay the insurer a little premium for organising that risk-pool. In practice, insurance has two major problems which, in the words of finance writer Matt Levine, "are so well known as to be cliches": adverse selection and moral hazard.

If our twin brother's dinner each night is a protein smoothie, and ours is meatballs pickled in cyanide, our probability of racking up vast health bills are different in ways that our insurer doesn't know about. (This is called "asymmetric information" — we know things about ourselves that the insurer doesn't, so our information is not symmetric.) The concern on the insurer's part is that asymmetric information will lead to bad outcomes for their firm: our healthy twin will look at the monthly premium being asked, compare it to his expected hospital spending, and realise that it's a terrible deal for him; meanwhile, we'll look at the exact same premium and see that for us it's a bargain. The insurer will suffer from **adverse selection**: only the worst (that is, "*adverse*") customers will *select* to buy insurance.

If adverse selection occurs, and only the costliest consumers (or as economists say, "lemons") sign up, then the prevailing price might not allow the insurance company to break even. And if the insurer raises the price to break even with a pool full of lemons, only the lemons will get their money's worth from buying insurance. Everyone else goes uninsured, despite wanting insurance if they could get it at a more reasonable price. The market breaks down due to insurees knowing more about their insurance risk than the insurers.

The second core problem for insurance is **moral hazard**: basically, the danger (to the insurer) that once you are insured against incurring a loss or bad outcome you'll be less careful about preventing it. Once we buy insurance for our phones, perhaps we'll be more willing to whip it out to take a photo while skydiving, because we know that if we drop it someone else is going to pay. (Perhaps the insurer can stipulate in the contract against a specific piece of stupidity like that, but they can never fully stop you from being more careless in unobservable ways once you know that someone else will help you pay for the damage.)

Again, Levine explains how in practice this risk is not always a reality: for example, "getting a big car-insurance payout doesn't help much if you die in the car crash," and more quotidianly most drivers don't want to deal with the hassle of claiming insurance, so people will still drive carefully even when insured. But it remains the case that, consciously or unconsciously, the fact of having bought insurance makes people behave more carelessly, because they won't bear the full burden for the consequences. Again, the insurance company may feel less inclined to offer insurance at attractive prices if it knows that once insured the risks go up.

The opportunity of big data in insurance lies in insurers knowing more and more about insurees, and thus reducing the asymmetric information problem, while the increasing ability of the insurer to "watch" the insuree (and the insuree's awareness that she's being watched) reduces the power of the moral hazard problem. In the age of AI, the producer's ability to know more about the consumer than she knows about herself fundamentally shifts the balance of power between them.

The Insurer Wants To Read Your Diary

Suppose you're a health insurer, and you face two broad groups of customers: (soon-to-be) sick ones and healthy ones. Insuring the sick is not (financially) smart for you: you already know they're sick (or that they likely will be, because they have a family history of Alzheimer's — or data from their fitbit tells you that they don't sleep well, which predicts Alzheimer's in later life), and will require expensive treatment, so in order to cover your expected costs you'd have to charge an absurdly, unaffordably high premium.

But it gets trickier than that: depending on how many sick and healthy people there are in the population, and the exact costs of paying for the treatment of the sick, it's possible that you can't even insure the *collective* mix of healthy and sick people. This is where the problem of adverse selection kicks in: if your insurance is priced to include the true cost of sick customers, healthy customers will balk at the premiums. (This is the logic behind government mandates forcing everyone to buy health insurance: by forcing the healthy to participate in the insurance market, you try to prevent a downward-spiral where only the sick buy insurance and therefore health insurance becomes unviable.)

However, if you're able to differentiate the sick and healthy customers, it might be economically viable to offer insurance to the healthy group against freak occurrences that are rare, unanticipated and out of each person's control. This is where economist-logic and public opinion diverge: economists generally think it's better for some people to have insurance than for nobody to have insurance, while public opinion is often sufficiently outraged at that kind of divergence that it would (in effect) prefer to create a situation where nobody is insured at all.

There's a "simple" solution to the adverse selection problem, but not everybody likes it: insurers can use big data for underwriting decisions. Our insurer couldn't historically know what we eat in the privacy of our home, or what weird and dangerous hobbies we have. But, today, if they partner with our credit card company, they can clearly see our excessive spending on deep-fried sugarcane, acrobatic ferrets and dangerous fireworks. As such, they can charge us a premium that actually incorporates the risk of insuring us... and we will still pay it, because in our heart of hearts we know that training stunt ferrets is a foolish endeavour that will not end well for us. Similarly, our aesthete twin's credit-card records will show that all his money is spent on broccoli, aerobics equipment, and incredibly wholesome turn-of-the-century novels; the AI-savvy insurer can offer him a premium low enough that he's actually willing to pay it (incidentally leaving him even more money to spend on broccoli, creating a weird but virtuous cycle).

Some Actors In Healthcare Don't (or Shouldn't) Care If It's Correlation Or Causation

Some actors in the healthcare system care deeply about causation. For example, if the government is considering an intervention to ban some product that's linked to bad health, it's very important to them to know whether the product *causes* the negative outcome or just happens to be used by people who tend to have the negative outcome anyway. Insurers, on the other hand, are in a different boat: in a lot of cases it doesn't matter to them whether the relationship between an activity and a health outcome is causal or not, so long as it can be used effectively to *predict* costs.

For example, in early 2019 the American health insurance giant Aetna started offering free Apple watches. There's no such thing as a free watch, and certainly not when it's coming from an insurance giant. So what's the catch? You might think it's just "you have to wear the watch and track your health for Aetna," which would make a certain amount of sense: Aetna gives you a watch and then "encourages" you to engage in trackable healthy behaviours, thereby lowering Aetna's future spending on your medical treatments. There is also talk about such data helping revolutionize medicine, encouraging healthier behavior, and so forth. And it's quite possible that this is why Aetna is doing it, or at least that this is what they think they're doing it for.

But there's also a simpler, and, perhaps more cynical, explanation. In order to participate in this plan, you have to *be the kind of person who is willing to wear a health-tracking watch and willing to believe that it improves your health outcomes, perhaps even without having seen evidence to that effect.* In this alternative story, the actual wearing and tracking is incidental.

In Chapter 3, we noted that AI doesn't understand causation: an AI model can't tell the difference between "owning a yacht causes you to live longer" and "the kind of person who owns a yacht is also the kind of person who will live longer for some reason other than the yacht." What we didn't mention was that some actors care deeply about causation, but others don't — or at least they can also be successful without. They only care so long as a factor has predictive power. If you're the government and you're trying to implement national health policy, before you give everyone in the country a yacht you need to know whether that actually *causes* longer life or only correlates with it. If you're a health insurer, though, it doesn't actually matter: if sticking "owns a yacht?" into your analysis helps you better predict longevity then you might be happy to do it, regardless of why it works. (Especially if that variable is easier and cheaper to come by than detailed data about what a certain individual eats, what their mental health is and so forth.)

Similarly, insurance companies want you to believe that their various "healthy lifestyle" inducements (discounted gym memberships, smart watches, sleep trackers and so on) are offered because the insurer wants to make you healthier — for the insurer's own profit, sure, but at least they want to make you healthier. From an economist's perspective, though, this isn't necessarily the case: the insurer doesn't have to make you healthier if it can just select for customers who are already inclined to good health. A customer willing and able to perform behaviours that are considered "pro-health" (vegetarianism, gym-going, wearing a smart watch and so on) is probably a good customer to have, whether or not these things actually have any effect on health at all. If your health insurance offers airline miles as a bonus for "good behavior" — our guess is that getting your dose of radiation by flying through the stratosphere isn't all that good for your health really; it's just a guess because after all neither of us is a "real doctor"

— then selecting people who like flying is probably a more important motivation than improving their health for these insurers.

To be fair, the insurance companies don't *have* to be that cynical — they could truly believe that the interventions improve a customer's health, the point is just that the interventions can be effective regardless. The insurer looks at the output of a big data analysis and sees that customers who regularly go to the gym have lower healthcare spending. It doesn't matter whether the insurer naively assumes this correlation is causative, cynically exploits a relationship that they suspect is just a selection effect, or just doesn't think about it either way. So long as it remains true that people who go to the gym regularly cost less to insure (i.e. so long as incentivising gym-going doesn't leave the insurer with a bunch of more-expensive customers who now happen to go the gym more), the insurer benefits whether or not the relationship is causal.

How To Trick Your Health Insurer

Physicists moving into the social sciences are said to often forget that, once the thing you're studying is humans, your subjects (by contrast to particles) are liable to react to your interventions by changing their beliefs about the future and thus their behaviour, thereby screwing up your plans. Every social policy has to struggle with the difficulty that, once it exists, the people it deals with will react to its existence and change their behaviour accordingly. So it's inevitable that the rise of AI-based decision-making has led to two big trends: humans trying to outwit AIs, economists trying to model such behavior, and even "Adversarial machine learning" systems that try to outwit AIs and deal with AIs trying to outwit them.

Here's how those trends play out in the insurance business. Suppose you know that your insurer is using an algorithm to calculate your premium, and you suspect that the algorithm is using data from your credit card, your FitBit and your Facebook account. What can you do? You *could* start paying for all your unhealthy purchases in cash, and start buying vegetables on your credit card, but this strategy might be both expensive and inconvenient (at which point it's not clear if you're tricking your health insurer, or whether they're tricking you into eating more vegetables).

Facebook might be a little easier: it costs very little time or effort to join health-related Facebook groups (and leave self-help groups for people with a family history of Alzheimers). Suddenly you abandon your group memberships in "Deep Fried Sugarcane Enthusiasts" and "I Like Playing With Fireworks LOL" to "I <3 Marathon Running" and "People Who Love Being Low Health Risks."

The FitBit is also gameable: perhaps you can tie it to your dog's leg and send it out for a walk, run it through a spin cycle in your washing machine, or jiggle it around in some other way that simulates walking without you actually having to go outside. (In China, you can buy ready-made machines for that express purpose.) We start to get into complicated territory here, though: your insurer can invalidate your insurance if you directly submit false information on an application, but if the insurer is basing your premium on your FitBit data without explicitly telling you so, can they really punish you for falsifying data that you didn't submit to them? We have no idea. This is one of the many areas of the law that will likely evolve very fast over the next decade or so.

Even more unfortunately for you as an individual, it's not necessarily possible to trick your insurer in a way that you'd find satisfying. Just because the insurer is using data to make bigger profits, doesn't mean they're necessarily doing it by offering better rates to lower-risk customers. For legal reasons, the rates themselves might be based on a limited set of accepted criteria, but the insurer can still profit from big data just by attracting the customers who are unusually low risk *within* each category. So your attempts to trick the system by joining the "I <3 Marathon Running" Facebook group might not get you a better *price* for health insurance, just lead to you seeing a lot more health insurance adverts by insurers trying to attract people like you... somewhere among all the new posts about marathons.

How Your Email Address Might Increase Your Premium

The car insurer Admiral got some bad publicity when it used AI insights to determine its rates. "Admiral hikes insurance costs for drivers using Hotmail email addresses," proclaimed the headline of an "exposé" in a well-known British tabloid. The company issued a statement saying that "certain domain names are associated with more accidents than others."

Perhaps the insurer had to say that: it's probably the most sympathetic option they have, from a bad set of possible choices. And, as we discussed in Chapter 5, it really is possible that users with a Hotmail email address are consistently more expensive to insure. But if you want to think like an economist, you have to realise that this isn't the only reason an insurer might charge more to drivers with a certain email domain. What other patterns might lead to the same outcome?

Well, for example, it could be that Hotmail users are equally-good drivers as Gmail users, but are worse at comparison-shopping and therefore less likely to go elsewhere to find a better deal, therefore making the optimal price to offer them just a little bit higher.

Relatedly, it could be simply that Hotmail drivers have a higher willingness to pay. If you go to a shop and see three different bottled waters at three different prices, you don't assume that the difference is that one of the waters costs a lot more to produce.

The water companies just know that certain demographics have a lot more money to spare, and a lot more willingness to spend it on water, so they design and advertise certain brands to appeal to wealthier customers and price them accordingly.

By the way, if your immediate reaction to the Hotmail insurance story was to think "Hotmail users are bad drivers" rather than "Hotmail users are wealthy people who are willing to pay more" that instinct may or may not be accurate, but it's once again a story about *human* intuition, domain knowledge and contextual thinking. As always, it's not the data alone that is meaningful: it's the data as viewed through the lens of your theories about the world. Keep that in mind the next time a data scientist proclaims that prediction makes notions of causality redundant, that theory is dead thanks to advances in empirical research, or when you see the next tabloid post about a celebrity opining that it is just a question of (a relatively short period of) time until thinking computers replace all jobs.

Refusing A Smartphone Gets You Pooled With Other Refusers

You might think that you can beat the system by simply avoiding, as far as possible, giving these companies your data: the only winning move is not to play. Some of our friends who actually work on AI refuse to own a smartphone because they know how the data is being used, which certainly makes us think twice when poking at our phones. But it's not clear our smartphone-less friends are much better off.

See, what happens if you rebel against all modern norms and just refuse to use a smartphone? Well, the result is not that the insurer gives up on classifying you: it's that the insurer pools you with all the other people who don't have a smartphone. Think (beyond your social circle) who they are, and whether you want to be in the same (credit, health, ...) risk pool with them. And this will go *especially* poorly for you in a country where the insurer is legally prevented from using, say, age in its calculation: if the insurer is allowed to use smartphone ownership but not age, then it might well use smartphone ownership as a *proxy* for age, and pool you with a group of people who are largely over 75. (Or the insurer might not think about proxies at all, but use a largely unexplainable deep learning mechanism, in which smartphone ownership ends up serving a similar function as age.)

Essentially, the attempt to opt out of the system only helps you *before* the system becomes too prevalent. You don't have to sign up for your insurer's free FitBit: few enough people have such a device that it's OK for now to get pooled with "people who don't have a FitBit." But this is just an illustration of how data-pooling is outside your individual control. Perhaps a decade from now almost-everyone with reasonably healthy life and sleep patterns *will* use a FitBit, and your refusal to use one will get you pooled with other "weird" holdouts. It's hard to beat the system when everyone is the system, because then rebelling against the system is itself a notable trait.

This takes us back to the very start of our book: the business of big data is the business of all of us, whether we like it or not.

Conclusion

We're writing this book at a strange moment in human and economic history. A wave is coming, and everybody sees it coming, but most people don't really know what to do about it. There's a lot of mystery and a lot of wishful (or panic-stricken) thinking on the topic. Hopefully, after reading this book, you feel ready to go out and surf the AI wave instead of drowning under it.

Our framework in this book has been built on some simple economic logic: the AI revolution took off because of the falling price of data and the positive feedback loops between big data, machine learning and highly-talented humans. Machines will now generally out-compete humans at "routine prediction" in the same way that machines have long out-competed humans at various kinds of physical labour, but this change will also create enormous opportunities for wise humans. The important opportunities — which companies to invest in, which fields to enter, which industries to disrupt — won't be *easy*, but they will be *simple*: "all" you need to do is strategically apply good theory to figure out how to make the most of AI.

The good news is that you have everything you need to prepare for the big data revolution sitting right between your shoulders. Creativity, empathy, ethics, contextual thinking, domain knowledge, intuition, prediction under constraints, good judgement: every one of these human skills actually *rises* in value thanks to AI, and they're also the exact skills you need to figure out how to make the most of AI.

How do you hone and harness those special human superpowers? Reading this book was a great decision, of course, but there's so much more to learn. If you can, try taking an online introductory course in Python, Machine Learning or Data Science. You don't have to become an expert, by any stretch, but just getting an intuitive feel for what AI can and can't do will leapfrog you beyond your peers who treat AI like some large carnivorous beast to be avoided at all costs. (We promise: it's much friendlier than it looks.) But don't study data science alone: millions already do that. Study data science but *combine* it with economic theory. Again, you don't need to become an expert economist to get a great deal of value: just be sure to learn the basics of demand and supply, complements and substitutes. (You might say we're biased, but we can particularly recommend taking courses on the topic at the Oxford Saïd Business School...)

The way that AI strengthens the value of uniquely human talents has, perhaps, counter-intuitive implications. It's long been a joke that studying philosophy and ethics is a path to thinking deeply and analytically about your own unemployment, but if this was ever true it isn't any more: the rise of AI creates immediate, important work for ethicists and ethical thinkers. The same is true for all kinds of skills that some have looked down on as being too "soft", but which are exactly the skills that will not become commoditised by the rise of AI. We can't put it better than Jack Ma, founder of Chinese internet heavyweight Alibaba: "In the industrial [era], you had to remember faster, you [had] to remember more, you [had] to calculate faster. These are the things machines can now do much better than you. We [have to] teach our kids how to be innovative, constructive and creative so they can survive in the AI period."

For better or worse, the world of big data business models we describe in this book *is* the new world of business. Our aim is not to judge it, but to understand and predict it; as a player in this economy, whether investor or entrepreneur or consumer or regulator, your job in the years ahead will be to decide how to respond to it. It's sad to say, but as things stand you won't have too much competition: very few people are thinking deliberately, systematically and strategically about how to respond to the age of AI. So if you take just one message away from this book, let it be "never stop thinking": after all, it's the most human strength you have.

Appendix: Chapter Summaries

As an aide to memory (and to help you find specific material when you return to this book in future), we're offering this structured summary of the key points from each segment of the book. The summary won't necessarily make sense if you haven't read the book yet, though.

Chapter 1 Summary: Why the AI Revolution Is Happening Right Now

- Current AI is extremely good at exactly one thing: routine prediction, i.e. finding patterns in data-rich environments where the past consistently predicts the future.

- AI-based routine prediction enables companies to accurately assess the effects of different strategies; to price discriminate between consumer segments; and to overcome asymmetric information.

- The current AI wave is just about machine learning working on big data for routine prediction, not the speculative technologies you might see in a movie or read in the newspaper.

- Big data was made possible by the fall in data storage prices, starting with a five-fold fall between 2010 and 2012 alone, and the rise of cellphones creating vast amounts of valuable data.

- Older machine learning techniques (and the AI business models they enable) became viable at scale due to positive feedback loop between cheap data storage, improvements in computation, and more talent entering the field.

Chapter 2 Summary: Your Rideshare App Is In The Data Business, Even If You Don't Know It

- When rideshare apps start offering banking services, that only makes sense once you understand that rideshare apps are really in the data business (and own valuable data about your social and personal life which traditional banks can't access).

- There are three phases to the AI revolution. First, disruptors use AI to reduce the cost of existing products and produce data as a side effect; Second, data becomes the competitive advantage and businesses may switch business plans after realising the value of their data; Third, data becomes the competitive advantage and businesses may switch business plans after realising the value of their data.

- The Lending Club used alternative data to achieve lower fraud and default rates than traditional banks, despite having a lower quality borrower base.

- Ford makes one-third of its profits from car loans; eventually, making and selling cars will become merely a prelude to data-gathering. The acquisition of electronic scooter company Spin makes sense from this perspective.

- Data is also the answer to the mystery of how bikeshare companies can make money despite losing money in their core business.

- Even running a sushi restaurant can turn into a data business: demand estimation for customers is initially used to determine staffing levels, but eventually becomes a core business in its own right

Chapter 3 Summary: Everything You Do Is Data, And All That Data Is Being Tracked

- The rise of AI dovetailed with the rise of smartphones; thousands of pieces of data are being collected about you all the time, including your hesitations and inactions and your interactions with the physical world.

- For example, location data can tell you companies where you spend your money; telecoms can often legally sell your location data without your permission.

- Vast amounts of your data — browser history, payments history and so on — might be publicly available without you realising it.

- Your email address, your device, how you input your email address, whether you use capital letters and so on all predict your probability of defaulting on a payment

- AI helps create markets where they weren't previously viable, e.g. making it possible to make small loans and differentiate safe and risky borrowers, and making it possible to advertise at very niche audiences

- AI also enables what economists call "price discrimination": charging each consumer specifically the maximum amount she is willing to pay, like a seller at a market haggling to find the right price

- Very few companies have the scale of data and the economic thinking skills to do this kind of work, but the ones that do make a lot of money from it.

Chapter 4 Summary: Don't Compete With AI At The Things It's Good At, Complement AI With The Things You're Good At

- If you were a farmer who hand-pulled a plough when the ox-plough was invented, you had three choices: move into a profession that ox can't do (like art), learn to harness an ox-team, or use your human intelligence to come up with creative new ways to deploy ox.
- Hairdressers will be safe from the AI wave because they're doing something AIs can't do: hairdressing is non-routine, and the human touch is really important. Meanwhile, cabbies who memorised the map of London will be outcompeted by AI, since this is a routine prediction task.
- Radiologists will be outcompeted at diagnosing tumours, but will be able to spend more time on human-only tasks like counselling and understanding patients; high Frequency Trading has been taken over by algorithms but Macro remains the domain of humans. The relevant analysis is not which "jobs" or "industries" will be replaced by AI, but which specific *tasks* are better suited to AI than to humans.
- Learning to code is a great career for those who truly enjoy it, but the greatest value from learning to code

might come from those who use the knowledge to manage how AI is applied.

Chapter 5 Summary: Super Humans, Or The Unique Human Intelligence Strengths That Complement AI

- Some of the best complements for AI: doing cutting edge AI research, managing teams of AI programmers, strategising which data to collect and which business models to develop, and thinking deeply about how humans can complement AI.

- Abraham Wald had a completely different theory to explain the same data of damaged planes coming back from World War II. His strong statistical reasoning and deep understanding of context let him come to better conclusions from the same data.

- AI can never decide when a structural break has happened and old data is no longer relevant. A big war, referendum, or election might be fundamentally similar to previous experiences or not; only a human can make that call. An AI can't advise you when not to use the AI.

- Cleaning and organising data is a big part of the work when doing big data projects. If you select (or remove) the wrong data the conclusions will be wrong.

- Humans are also needed to distinguish cause and effect. AI Bots price second-hand books at absurd prices because they don't understand causality or context.

Chapter 6 Summary: How Law And Ethics Constrain AI Business Models

- Law, regulation and ethics set limits on which kinds of data-driven business models are actually viable.

- More-detailed targeting means more lucrative ad-sales; Facebook and Google and Amazon dominate digital advertising because they have the richest customer data. Legal constraints set limits on data bundling and data targeting.

- Pooling data from multiple sources is even more valuable than those sources on their own; Google and Mastercard partnered up to tie online ads to in-store sales.

- Facebook wants to combine its data with WhatsApp and Instagram, creating a new frontier in competition regulation (entirely separate from the privacy regulation).

- France has banned AIs from analysing judicial decisions to find patterns in judge's decisions, something that human lawyers have done for years. The coming years will be particularly sensitive since specific AI applications can be crushed before they grow.

- COMPAS, an AI used to predict recidivism, was accused of being unfair towards black defendants but, ultimately, it is actually impossible to create an algorithm that is fair by all reasonable criteria.

Chapter 7 Summary: Are Insurance Markets About To Self-Destruct?

- The insurance market suffers from two big problems: adverse selection (people who are a bigger risk in invisible ways select into buying more insurance) and moral hazard (people behave more carelessly and riskily once they have insurance).

- AI creates opportunities for un-pooling customers and charging each individual a personalised premium, with all the ethical dilemmas that suggests.

- Insurers can benefit from offering "healthy products" such as smart watches and gym memberships if those help attract more low-risk customers, regardless of whether the products actually contribute to better health.

- You can try to trick your health insurer through your spending and social habits, but it might not help you: instead of getting lower premiums, you might just get more health insurance ads.

- Higher car insurance premiums for Hotmail users don't necessarily mean Hotmail users are worse drivers: they might just be worse comparison shoppers, or have higher willingness to pay.

- Refusing to own a smartphone to avoid having data collected about you doesn't necessarily save you, because then you just get pooled with non-smartphone-owners.

Recommended Reading

As economists, we believe in the power of complements: the following books will help you get more out of *The Business Of Big Data*, as much as *The Business Of Big Data* will help you get more out of the following books:

- *Prediction Machines*, by Ajay Agrawal, Joshua Gans, and Avi Goldfarb. A focussed look at AI as "a drop in the cost of [routine] prediction" and substitutes and complements in the decision making process.
- *Stand Out Of Our Light*, by James Williams. An illuminating philosophical analysis of the attention-grabbing nature of social media, and how user attention creates data.
- *21 Lessons For The 21st Century*, by Yuval Noah Harari. A big-picture analysis of where AI will take our societies, and how humans must respond to stay relevant.

For further details and recommendations, please visit our website: www.thebusinessofbigdata.com

Acknowledgments

Martin would like to acknowledge Sandra Fredman, Mao Ye, and Moritz Hardt.

Uri would like to acknowledge Toby Mundy, Arvind Srinivasan, Kaamya Sharma, Dua Hassan, Joel Shor, Josh Franklin, Steph Wykstra, Jesse Dunietz, Tony Hu, Stephen Fox, Audrey Low, Alex Linsley, Joelle Ní Ghruagáin, Matt Molteno, Lev Konstantinovskiy, and Mogs Lieu.

Uri and Martin would like to acknowledge Jacob Silkstone, our editor, and Natalie Harney, our cover designer, without whom this book would have been very much uglier in two different senses.

ENDNOTES

Chapter 1

"we consider particular signs of intelligence..." *The Limits of Formal Learning*, Nautilus, David Chapman, 11 September 2016.

"I like the idea of using artificial intelligence..." *Charlie Munger, Bill Gates On Future Of Artificial Intelligence*, CNBC, 2 May 2016.

"The foundations of modern..." Joel Shor, August 2019.

Falling cost of data chart: after *Hard Drive Cost Per Gigabyte*, Andy Klein, Backblaze, 11 July 2017.

Chapter 2

"to put to work its vast trove of user data..." *Didi Chuxing moves into financial services*, Financial Times, 2 January 2019.

"affluent and represent a quality segment..." *Chinese ride-hailing giant Didi Chuxing enters financial services amid profit push*, Sarah Dai, South China Morning Post, 3 January 2019.

"more than half of..." *To the Cloud and Beyond: Big Data in the Age of Machine Learning*, Harvard Business Review, 4 August 2017.

Chapter 3

"Customers [whose email]...", "There are [few]...", "For example..." *On the Rise of FinTechs – Credit Scoring Using Digital Footprints*, Berg et al, Irish Finance Working Paper Series, 15 July 2019.

Chapter 5

"data seldom..." *A Nobel- winning economist's tips for how to deal with a more uncertain world*, Quartz, Allison Schrager, 24 November 2018.

"80% of the work with an AI project..." *Data Challenges Are Halting AI Projects, IBM Executive Says*, Wall Street Journal, Jared Council, 28 May 2019.

"If you want to be a good data scientist..." Twitter, Nate Silver, 6 October 2019.

Chapter 6

"Today's big tech companies have too much..." *Here's how we can break up Big Tech*, Elizabeth Warren, 8 March 2019.

"the alternative, frankly, is..." *Zuckerberg: The Recode interview*, Kara Swisher, 8 October 2018.

"the identity data of magistrates..." *France Bans Judge Analytics, 5 Years In Prison For Rule Breakers*, Artificial Lawyer, 4 June 2019.

Chapter 7

"are so well known..." and "getting a big car-insurance..." *Lyft's IPO Was a Little Awkward*, Bloomberg, Matt Levine, 7 May 2019.

"Admiral hikes insurance costs..." *Admiral hikes insurance costs for drivers using Hotmail email addresses*, The Sun, Katie Hodge and Ben Leo, 23 January 2018

Conclusion

"In the industrial..." *Why Jack Ma says he'd never get a job at Alibaba today*, CNBC, Karen Gilchrist, 20 October 2019.

For further notes and references, please visit www.thebusinessofbigdata.com

ABOUT THE AUTHORS

Martin Schmalz is an Associate Professor of Finance at the University of Oxford's Saïd Business School. He previously taught at the University of Michigan's Stephen M. Ross School of Business and was featured as one of the "40 under 40" best business school professors worldwide at the age of 33; he holds an 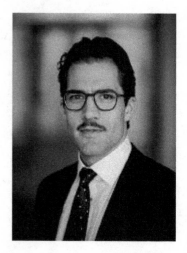 M.A. and PhD in Economics from Princeton University.

Martin's research has been published in The Journal of Finance, Journal of Financial Economics, and Review of Financial Studies and has been covered, among others, by The New York Times, The Economist, Wall Street Journal, Financial Times, Bloomberg, The New Yorker, The Atlantic, Forbes and Fortune. He was invited to present to regulators and policy makers across the globe, including the US Department of Justice, The White House Council of Economic Advisers, European Commission and the European Parliament.

Uri Bram is the author of *Thinking Statistically*, which was selected by *Personal MBA's* Josh Kaufman as one of the 99 best business books ever written, and has been translated  into Korean and Mandarin. Uri was the *Economics of Everyday Life* columnist at the Economist's 1843 magazine, and is the publisher of *the Browser* and *the Listener* curation newsletters. As a statistician and economist Uri has consulted for leading international organisations including the World Bank. As a developer, his sites and apps have reached over 500k people. He helped write the documentation for Google's TensorFlow-GAN library.

For more information, please visit our website:
www.thebusinessofbigdata.com

Or contact us:
uri@thebusinessofbigdata.com
martin@thebusinessofbigdata.com

CPSIA information can be obtained
at www.ICGtesting.com
Printed in the USA
LVHW101120100123
736776LV00004B/619